Paul Fos

THE
ESOTERIC KEYS
OF
ALCHEMY

Ishtar Publishing
Vancouver

ESOTERIC KEYS OF ALCHEMY
AN ISHTAR PUBLISHING BOOK: 0-9780535-1-6
978-0-9780535-1-2

PRINTING HISTORY
Ishtar Publishing edition published 2006

1 3 5 7 9 10 8 6 4 2

Ishtar Publishing
141-6200 McKay Ave
Suite 716
Burnaby, BC
Canada V5H4M9

www.ishtarpublishing.com

Printed and bound in the United States.

Esoteric Keys of Alchemy is one of the best modern books on alchemy that we have seen. It is with great pride and pleasure that we present this book to the occult community and to all those who follow the work of Paul Foster Case.

CONTENTS

	PAGE
WHAT ALCHEMY REALLY IS	1
THE FIRST MATTER	25
THE FIRST MATTER II	51
THE THREE PRINCIPLES	75
THE ELEMENT OF FIRE	99
THE ELEMENT OF WATER	123

I
WHAT ALCHEMY REALLY IS

*W*ebster's International Dictionary defines alchemy as: "The medieval chemical science, whose great objects were the transmutation of the baser metals into gold, and the discovery of the universal cure for diseases and means of indefinitely prolonging life." This, the commonly accepted exoteric definition of alchemy, gives a partial and therefore distorted idea of the significance of Hermetic science and practice. Our first lesson will therefore be devoted to a consideration of the true meaning of the Hermetic doctrine, its real objects, and the field of its practical operations.

The literature of alchemy is difficult because it is intentionally cryptic. Alchemical authors use a complicated and obscure system of symbolism. They continually resort to blinds, enigmas, cryptograms, and other devices intended to conceal their real meaning from uninitiated readers. Never do they actually lie, but it has been said that when they seem to speak most openly, the wary reader should be most ready to suspect a hidden meaning.

The difficulty of getting at the real import of the alchemical literature is further increased by the fact that there are three distinct classes of alchemical books. The first contains the works of the true sages, who were in the chain of the oral tradition of Hermetic science. The second class consists of books written by persons who misunderstood the writings of the genuine adepts, and supposed them to be explanations of purely physical processes having to do with the modification and transmutation of ordinary metals by means of crude chemical experiments. The third class comprises many volumes written by charlatans and pretenders, who took advantage of popular interest in alchemy to line their pockets at the expense of their dupes.

Fortunately, the oral tradition of Hermeticism has never died out. It is because the School of Ageless Wisdom has become a link in the chain of that tradition that we are able to present this body of knowledge concerning the inner secrets of Hermeticism. We posses the keys to the cryptic symbols of the adepts. We shall use them to give you a clear exposition of the teaching, free from the intentional concealments which were necessary in less enlightened ages.

We know that our claim will be ridiculed by the world. It will be denied, too, by some who have established themselves in the public eye as authorities, by reason of their voluminous commentaries and exposition upon occult and mystical topics. The fact remains that the alchemical teaching given here is by no means the opinion of one person, or group of persons, arrived at after the perusal of ancient tomes. As in our expositions of Tarot and Rosicrucianism, what we give you here is a faithful transmission of instruction received from the Inner School, and confirmed by our own personal experience. Whether you accept it as such just now is not the important thing. We know that if you put this instruction to the tests of reason, intuition, and practice, you will be able to demonstrate its truth beyond the shadow of a doubt. Furthermore, if you carry the work to its final stages, you will be able to make your own personal contact with the adepts of the Inner School.

The bulk of alchemical literature now extant was written during the Middle Ages, but the beginnings of the Hermetic science and practice may be traced to a much earlier period. For example, a fundamental tenet of alchemy is the declaration of the *Emerald Tablet*: "That which is below is as that which is above, and that which is above is as that which is below, for the performance of the miracles of the

One Thing." There can be little doubt that the *Emerald Tablet*, as we have it, is a relatively modern work, although it is attributed to Hermes Trismegistus; but exactly the same doctrine is taught in the *Hindu Katha Upanishad*: "As below so above, as above so below; he passes from death to death who finds here the least shadow of variety. There is no variety in THAT. It should be grasped by the mind alone. He, indeed, passed from death to death who here finds the least shadow of variety."

Swami Vivekananda writes,

> In India there was a sect called the Rasayanas. Their idea was that ideality, knowledge, spirituality and religion were all very right, but that the body was the only instrument by which to attain to all these. If the body broke now and then it would take so much more time to attain the goal. For instance, a man wants to practice Yoga, or wants to become spiritual. Before he has advanced very far he dies. Then he takes another body and begins again, then dies, and so on, and in this way much time will be lost in dying and being born again. If the body could be made strong and perfect, so that it would get rid of birth and death, we should have more time to become spiritual. So these Rasayanas say, first make the body very strong, and they claim that this body can be made immortal. Their idea is that if the mind is manufacturing the body, and if it be true that each mind is only one particular outlet to that infinite energy, and that there is no limit to each particular outlet getting any amount of power, why is it impossible that we should keep our bodies all the time? We shall have to manufacture all the bodies we shall ever have. As soon as this body dies we shall have to manufacture another. If we can do that why cannot we do that just here and now, without getting out? The theory is perfectly correct. If it is possible that we live after death, and make other bodies, why is it impossible that we should have the power of making bodies here, without entirely dissolving this body, simply changing it continually? They also

thought that in mercury and in sulfur was hidden the most wonderful power, and that by certain preparations of these a man could keep the body as long as he liked. (*Raja Yoga*, pages 207-208)

So long ago as 1879, Dr. William A. P. Martin, a missionary to China, published an article in the *China Review*, in which he offered evidence to show that alchemy was known and practiced in China at least three hundred years before the Christian Era, and that it entered Europe by way of Byzantium and Alexandria. He cited many ancient texts, which include the following points of similarity between Chinese alchemical literature and that of the West:

(1) The doctrine that there is a seed of metals;

(2) The idea that there is in all things an active principle whereby they may attain to a condition of higher development;

(3) The fact that alchemy was perpetuated in China chiefly by oral tradition, supplemented by books written in figurative language;

(4) Chinese alchemy, like that of Europe, is inseparable from astrology and magic;

(5) The combination of the idea of the transmutation of metals with that of the making of a universal medicine;

(6) The secret of making gold was regarded as being inferior to that of the Elixir of Life;

(7) Success in the work required self-culture and self-discipline;

(8) The metals were all regarded as being composite;

(9) The true matters of the work were concealed by names also used in the West, including lead, mercury, sulfur, and cinnabar;

(10) The same symbolic terms appear in Chinese as in

Western alchemical texts- such as, the "Radical Principle," the "Green Dragon," the "True Mercury," the "True Lead," and so on;

(11) There were two alchemical processes, the first inward and spiritual, the second outward and material, and there were two elixirs, a greater and a lesser.

We have condensed this account of Dr. Martin's essay from A.E. Waite's *Secret Tradition in Alchemy*. Mr. Waite is obliged to include it in his book, because it cannot be ignored, but he does what he can to minimize its importance. This, because the evidence conflicts more or less with his thesis- which is that the bulk of alchemical writings are the product of sordid lust for gold, written by deluded men who had in view no other end than the hope of sudden wealth. As usual, Mr. Waite is an indefatigable and successful miner for facts and information, but his every page demonstrates his lack of the keys of oral tradition which unlock the treasure houses of Ageless Wisdom.

The Western literature of alchemy can be traced back to the days when Alexandria was the meeting place for that group of adepts of the Inner School who later transferred their activities to Fez, and from that city issued the earliest versions of Tarot. In much of its doctrine, the Hermetic and alchemical philosophy is definitely Neo-Platonic, and as Neo-Platonism is tinged with ideas brought to Alexandria by wandering teachers from India, we can understand how there came to be a mixture of Hindu thought, Egyptian Magic, and Greek Philosophy in the Hermetic teaching set forth in the symbols of alchemy and Tarot.

Authorities disagree as to the derivation of the noun *alchemy*. Plutarch supposed it to be a combination of the Arabic definite article *Al* with the Greek *Chumeia*, signifying "to pour." An opinion prevailing today is that the true derivation is from *Khem*, an Egyptian noun meaning "black, fertile soil," in contrast to the barren sand. *Khem* was the name given by Egyptians to their country, and even Plutarch knew this, for he mentions it in his *Isis and Osiris*. The derivation of alchemy from *Khem* is further confirmed by the fact that old alchemical books allude to Hermetic practice as "the Egyptian Art."

The esoteric doctrine received by us is that the noun *alchemy*, like many other words in the Western literature of Hermetic science, is derived from Hebrew. It does not follow from this that alchemy is of Hebrew origin. Rather should it be understood that for certain purposes the Inner School adopted the Chaldean-Hebrew language to preserve and transmit esoteric doctrines, just as modern scientists use Latin and Greek for similar purposes.

In Hebrew the word is אלחמה. It is a combination of the Semitic god-name אל, *EL*, signifying "strength," with חמה, *Khammaw*, the Hebrew poetical noun for "Sun." Thus "alchemy" may be interpreted as meaning "strength of the sun," or "God the Sun." Both interpretations are in harmony with alchemical doctrine.

Because חמה, *Khammaw*, is derived from the root חם, *Khem*, "the black one," which, as we have said, was given by the Egyptians to their own country, and by Egyptian priests to a certain aspect of the father-god, Osiris, alchemy is truly the Egyptian Art, and it is also the Science of God, the Black One, that is, the Hidden One. It is the science of the hidden essence which is veiled by solar energy. It is also the Osirian Art, because it is the system of practice which enables us to control the hidden powers of the "underworld" which, according to the Egyptian doctrine, is governed by Osiris. This hidden realm of Osiris is the world of occult forces and laws concealed beneath the superficial appearances of the world which is perceived by the greater number of human beings.

As this lesson is intended for affiliates of the School of Ageless Wisdom who have had the preliminary training given in the Basic Tarot course, we may also apply to the word אלחמה the knowledge to be gained from the Tarot Keys. Thus we find that the Hebrew letters of the word correspond to the following Tarot sequence:

LETTERS:	ה	מ	ח	ל	א
KEY NOS.:	4	12	7	11	0

This may be read in many ways, and you should try to find readings for yourself. Here is one: (א:0) Alchemy is the art of using the Life-Breath in accordance with the fundamental postulate that no matter how far the physical manifestation of that Life-Breath may have been carried by evolution, further progress is always possible. (ל:11) In the practice of this art, one of the great secrets is that of the balance of forces by their opposites, hence it is written that equilibrium is the basis of the Great Work. (ח:7) Furthermore, alchemical practice is made possible by the fact, alluded to in our quotation from Vivekananda, that each personal mind is one particular outlet to infinite energy—that is to say, that every person is a "House of Influence," receiving and specializing the currents of inexhaustible celestial energy. (מ:12) This being rightly understood, it becomes evident that the business of the alchemist has much to do with the reversal of the mental attitudes and ways of life followed by the masses. (ה:4) Finally, alchemy aims at nothing less than complete control over all physical conditions, because its object is to make the personal mind an unobstructed channel for the Constituting Intelligence which already exercises precisely that control.

By adding the numbers of the foregoing Keys, we get

thirty-four, and since there is no Tarot Key bearing that number, we add the digits and get seven. Thus we learn from the Key numbers corresponding to the letters of אלחמה that the essential meaning of the word is summed by Key Seven, The Chariot. In this connection it is interesting to note that one of the celebrated alchemical texts is named *The Triumphal Chariot of Antimony*. It is one of the subtlest of alchemical books because it teaches the spiritual side of the art while at the same time devoting much space to the medicinal and other virtues of the actual metal antimony. Its author, Basil Valentine, clearly indicates his knowledge of the doctrine conveyed by Key Seven, in his instructions concerning the preparation of the student for laboratory practice, wherein he recommends:

> Invocation of God, with a certain heavenly intention, drawn from the depths of a sincere heart and conscience, liberated from ambition, hypocrisy and all other vices which are in affinity with these, including arrogance, boldness, luxury, petulancy, oppression of the poor, and similar evils. All these are to be eradicated from the heart, that when a man desires to prostate himself before the Throne of Grace, in order to obtain health, he may do so with a conscience free from unprofitable weeds, *so that his body may be transmuted into a holy temple of God and purged from all uncleanness.*

By numeration of letters, אלחמה is eighty-four, and this is a significant number because it is 7 x 12, indicating the working of the seven alchemical metals or planets through their twelve spheres of manifestation, which are represented in astrology by the twelve signs of the zodiac. We shall come to these metals and their real meaning before the end of the lesson.

Furthermore, in Qabalah the number 84 represents

these words: אגף *Aggaph*, a chosen troop; דמם, *Dammam*, was silent; חלום, *Khalome*, a dream; חנוך, *Enoch*, signifying "initiation"; and ידע, *Yawda*, to know. The slightest acquaintance with alchemical literature suffices to show that the adepts of Hermetic science are indeed a chosen troop; that they maintain strict silence as to the innermost secrets of the art from all who have not proved their fitness to receive that instruction; that one of their ways of communication is through direct action upon that mode of human consciousness which forms the imagery of our dreams; that Hermetic science is the essence of what is taught in all systems of initiation; and, finally, that this science is not mere speculation or theory, but definite and demonstrable knowledge. Thus you may see that even the name of this ancient art, when interpreted in accordance with ancient occult methods, gives a clear statement of what alchemy really is.

Alchemy, then is misunderstood if it be thought to be no more than a crude precursor of modern chemistry. Its true adepts sought other results than those aimed at by the modern chemist. The instruments of their work had nothing in common with the apparatus of our laboratories. True, they described such apparatus. They even published illustrations of it in some of their books. They did so as part of their plan to prevent uninitiated readers from discovering their real secret. For, as we have already said, the alchemical books were written as supplements to oral instruction. They were aids to memory, rather than complete expositions of Hermetic practice. Thus they were so arranged that none but those who were duly and truly prepared might guess the real meaning from a perusal of their strange, cryptic pages.

The Hermetic art has to do with process carried out in a *hidden* laboratory. In the works of genuine adepts, the vessels of the art are invariably described as being *secret*. So are the processes. Thus Bernard of Trevisan writes: "Dissolution is the whole mystery of the art, and is to be accomplished, not as some have thought, by means of fire, *but in a wholly abstruse manner*, by the help of Mercury." Here the adjective "abstruse" has the now obsolete meanings: "concealed, or hidden."

Thomas Charnocke gives a hint to the same effect when he says, in his *Breviary*: "I think few potters within this realm have made at any time such cunning ware, as we for our science do fashion and prepare."

Can anything be plainer than this continual repetition of such words as *secret, hidden, abstruse*? Even the adjective "Hermetic" has come to have this meaning, as when we say that a vessel is "hermetically sealed." Alchemical practice is primarily an interior operation.

At the same time, although we have said that alchemy is not crude chemistry, and that all its instruments are contained in a hidden laboratory, you must not jump to the conclusion that it is a pure metaphysical process. It may be correctly described as being a psycho-physiological operation. The Hermetic practice is a method of psychological transformation directed by the conscious mind of man. This is the mode of human consciousness personified by the Egyptians as Thoth, by the Greeks as Hermes, and by the Romans as Mercury. Thus it becomes evident that what Bernard of Trevisan means by saying that the operation is performed by the help of Mercury is little more than a paraphrase of what we have quoted from the *Katha Upanishad*: "It should be grasped by the mind alone."

Dissolution is said to be the whole mystery of alchemy, because Hermetic practice enables us to control those functions of our bodies which dissolve, or break down into their constituent elements, the forms of materials taken from our environment. The laboratory of the alchemist is his own personality. The secret vessels therein are organs in his own physical body, together with their astral and etheric counterparts.

The principle piece of alchemical apparatus is a furnace, called an "athanor." Eliphas Levi says,

> We are all in possession of the chemical instrument, the great and sole athanor which answers for the separation of the subtle from the gross and the fixed from the volatile. This instrument, complete as the world and precise as mathematics, is represented by the sages under the emblem of the pentagram, or five-pointed star, which is the absolute sign of human intelligence. I will follow the example of the wise by forbearing to name it; it is too easy to guess it.

Today there is no need for even the slight concealment which seemed advisable when Levi wrote. The athanor is the human organism. Its name, like many other alchemical terms, is derived from Hebrew. In that language it is *Ath-Ha-Nour*, which means "Essence of Fire." Thus Bernard of Trevisan is correct when he says that the Great Work is not performed by means of fire, and so are the other sages who insist that the fire employed by them is "no common fire." It is the essence of fire, manifested as the human organism, which provides us with the instrument for the Great Work. Hence the athanor is defined as a "self-feeding, digesting furnace, in which an equable heat is maintained." Is not this a fairly good description of the human body?

Some references to the significance of the pentagram have been made in other publications of the School of Ageless Wisdom, notably in Lessons 44 to 48 of B.O.T.A. Second Year Course. It is intended, however, to publish as soon as possible a series of texts on magic, in which the arcane meaning of this august symbol will be fully dealt with.

For the present it is enough to say that Levi's own interpretation of the pentagram includes these two points: (1) that the five-pointed star is a figure of the human body; (2) that it expresses the mind's domination over the elements. Here he plainly states the Hermetic position, which is the same as that of the Hindu adepts mentioned by Swami Vivekananda. The mind of man can, and does, dominate all the forces of nature, through the instrumentality of the body. Hence the primary work of the alchemist is directed toward the purification and perfection of this chemical instrument.

It is perfectly true that the alchemist seeks to transmute the baser metals into gold. When he speaks of the seven metals, however, he means something other than the common products of the mine. Thus George Ripley warns his readers, in his *Compound of Alchemie*, against fruitless experiments with various substances, including "meane Mettalls dygged out of the Myne." And the other sages make the same distinction, speaking always of "our" Mercury, "our" Sulfur, "our" Gold and Silver, so as to make it plain that they are mentioning something peculiar to the Hermetic operation. The alchemical metals bear the names of the Sun, Moon, and the five planets known to the ancients, as follows:

METAL	PLANET	PLANETARY SYMBOL
Lead	Saturn	♄
Iron	Mars	♃
Tin	Jupiter	♂
Gold	Sol or Sun	☉
Copper (Brass)	Venus	♀
Silver	Luna or Moon	☿
Quicksilver	Mercury	☽

In many alchemical texts and formulas, the astrological symbols of the heavenly bodies names above are used to represent the metals. Elsewhere in the instruction issued by the School of Ageless Wisdom we have explained the correspondence of these planets to seven "interior stars" located within the human organism. The seven stars are the same as the seven chakras, or lotuses, of the Yoga philosophy. They have been identified with seven centers of the human nervous system, as follows:

PLANET	CHAKRA
Saturn	Sacral Plexus
Mars	Prostatic Ganglion
Jupiter	Solar Plexus
Sol or Sun	Cardiac Plexus
Venus	Pharyngeal Plexus
Luna or Moon	Pituitary Body
Mercury	Pineal Body

The transmutation of the baser metals into gold is the process whereby the vibratory action of these interior stars is so modified that the lower rates of vibration are transmuted, (literally, "changed across") and sublimated, or lifted up. This transmutation of the subtle force which works through the seven interior stars or alchemical metals has a triple consequence. It lends to spiritual illumination. It enables the perfect adept to exercise power which remains latent in most men. It gives him perfect bodily health.

The adept's health is the result of the perfect combination of all the chemical and electrical energies whose coordinated activities maintain the form and functions of his physical body. This state of radiant vitality is communicable. When it is attained, the alchemist can project his own rate of vibration upon other persons, and by inducing a similar rate in their etheric bodies, can heal their diseases. The alchemist's mental and spiritual vibration is also communicable. By projecting his own state of consciousness upon the mind of another, he can raise the level of that person's consciousness. Of such spiritual contagion there are many examples in the Bible, and in the sacred writings of other nations.

An actual force is projected. The alchemists call it the power of projection, by means of which, they say, the baser metals may be changed into gold. But Ripley warns us against misuse of the power. He points out that the metals upon which projection is made must first be properly cleansed.

What is meant is obvious when we understand the figurative language of alchemy. The work of projection refers to the transmutation of the minds and bodies of the adept's disciples. Upon this projection the perfection of the art depends, and it is by this projection of an unwritten something from the consciousness of one who knows to the mind of a properly prepared pupil that the inner secret of alchemy is transmitted, for it is never committed to writing. Indeed, it cannot be, for it goes beyond words.

Alchemy, then, aims at a state of consciousness which is reflected into the physical plane as perfect vibratory equilibrium. That equilibrium already exists in nature, and it is the business of the alchemist to manifest it through his own personality. Thus we are told that equilibrium is the basis of the Great Work, and admonished by all books on Hermetic practice to "imitate nature."

The higher, perfectly balanced state of personality is none other than the "new mind" of the injunction: "Be ye transformed by the renewing of your mind." It is a new understanding of life, based upon a new kind of first-hand experience.

A prominent characteristic of this experience is that

it is permeated with the quality of *eternity*, hinted at in the Rosicrucian inquiry: "Were it not an excellent thing to live always so as if you had lived from the beginning of the world, and should still live to the end thereof?"

Yet alchemy is not exclusively concerned with consciousness. What is aimed at in the performance of the Great Work is more than a belief, more than a state of mind, more than a metaphysical realization. When we say that the Great Work unfolds a new kind of consciousness, we mean you to understand that he in whom this unfoldment takes place is thereby enabled to express all the powers that go with it. He does actually find himself able to command the spirits of the elements, the subtle forces whose interplay of activity produces all the appearances of the physical world. This command enables him to transform his corruptible body into a body incorruptible. By this same mastery he also exerts over the physical forms in his environment such control that he can alter their appearance, and even change their atomic structure, by raising or lowering their rates of vibration. Thus the alchemical mastery does, in the end, enable its adepts to perform actual physical transmutations.

A great stumbling-block in the way of would-be alchemists is that so few of them perceive that man himself is the *primary* subject of the art. No secret formula can enable you to control the processes of nature unless you being by learning to control them within yourself. Your mind must be changed, so that you perceive and understand things hidden from the uninitiated. Your body must be changed, too, before you may safely employ it to specialize and transmit the high-tension currents of the Essence of Fire, which would destroy the physical organism of the average person.

Thus it is evident that alchemy is not, as some have supposed, merely a curious veil for religious mysticism.

It is that some alchemists have been mystics, like Jacob Boehme and Thomas Vaughan. It is true also that certain alchemical writings lend themselves easily to such a moral interpretation as was attempted by General Ethan Allen Hitchcock when he wrote his *Remarks on Alchemy and the Alchemists*. Concerning this book, A.E. Waite justly says: "It renders alchemical literature ridiculous by representing it as veiling in allegory and illustrating by symbols the most familiar principles of ethics, the ordinary laws of conduct and counsels of thinking in the heart- in other words, the daily matters of public teaching, not only by schoolmen and theologians, but by mendicant friars in the booths and marketplaces."

Mrs. Atwood's Suggestive Inquiry into the *Hermetic Mystery*, originally printed in 1850, only to be withdrawn in a few weeks because its author feared she had said too much, and then republished in 1920, after her death, offers yet another interpretation. Mrs. Atwood's thesis is that the alchemical operation is none other than the procedure we know today as hypnosis or mesmerism. She made a valiant attempt to defend her position, and her book is interesting, but not convincing, even to those who have not entered into the chain of the oral tradition. She and her father believed that the First Matter of the alchemist was identical with the magnetic fluid postulated by Mesmer to account for his cures. They were convinced that the alchemical process was a method for separating this subtle vital fluid from the gross body of man. By this means they believed it possible to heal diseases, awaken clairvoyant powers, and raise the consciousness of the mesmeric subject to higher levels.

As a variant of this interpretation, S. Foster Damon, in an article published some years since in the *Occult Review*, advanced the opinion that the First Matter of the alchemists is the ectoplasm supposed to be the basis of spirit materializations. He reached this view from his study of the writings of Thomas Vaughan.

Now, the three interpretations cited above have all some part of the truth. The observance of certain fundamental ethical principles is insisted upon by all genuine Hermetic authors. The Great Work does include practices akin to those of Mesmer, although they are far in advance of his inadequate technique. It may even be admitted that the First matter is the substance employed by genuine mediums for the production of their phenomena, although it should be noted that to admit this is not quite the same as to say that the First matter is ectoplasm.

The fact is that alchemy is really a Western variation of what Hindus call Yoga. This point we shall endeavor to make clear in the remaining pages of this lesson.

We have already called attention to the identity between the alchemical metals and the chakras of the Yoga system. We have also shown the remarkable similarity of thought and expression between the *Emerald Tablet* and a passage from the *Katha Upanishad*. We may continue these parallels considerably beyond these beginnings.

Fundamental in Hermetic science is the doctrine that all things whatsoever are manifestations of three principles, called Sulfur, Mercury, and Salt. They are not the common physical substances. Their names indicate three ways in which the One Thing manifests itself. One of these may be identified by a quality *like* a quality possessed by sulfur. Another has characteristics like those of quicksilver. The third has properties which resemble those of salt.

Sulfur or brimstone burns easily, and has choking fumes. It has been associated for centuries with the fires of hell, and with the seething passions which those fires typify. Mercury is liquid and flowing, and the surface of each globule of this metal is a mirror reflecting its environment. Its rapid movement, like that of a living creature, accounts for the name quicksilver, in which "quick" means both living and rapid, as we may see from the French *argent vive*, literally, "living silver." Salt crystallizes in perfect cubes, which have been types of earth since the time of Pythagoras; and its property is to arrest dissolution, or disintegrative chemical change. The quality of sulfur, then, is fiery and passionate. That of mercury is vital and reflective. That of salt is arrestive and binding.

Compare these alchemical doctrines with Yoga teaching. Hindu philosophers declare that three qualities, or *gunas*, enter into the composition of all things. Wherever there is a form, there are the three qualities. Their names are *Sattva*, *Rajas*, and *Tamas*. In the fourteenth chapter of the Bhagavad Gita, the characteristics of these three qualities are fully described. There we are told that *Rajas* is the embodiment of desire, and the producer of thirst and relish; that it ties the ego through attachment to action; that from it are born such things as greed, initiation of action, energy in great worldly achievements, unrest, and thirst. We learn also that *Sattva* is illuminative; that it is transparent, or light-transmitting, that it ties the ego through attachment to happiness and knowledge; that when it is dominant there is the illumination of knowledge at every gate of the body, and thus the senses and faculties attain the fullest manifestation of power. Finally, *Tamas* is said to be born of insensibility; to tie up the ego by means of heedlessness, laziness, sleep; to veil the power of discrimination; to be the cause of spiritual blindness. We might represent these three qualities by the three English words: Desire-force (*Rajas*); Intelligence (*Sattva*); Inertia (*Tamas*). The same three words could be used in place of sulfur, mercury, and salt.

Again, the alchemists recognize five underlying phases of manifestation, or five classes of expression for the One Thing. The first of these is the Quintessence, or Fifth Es-

sence, so named because it is a fifth thing, extracted in
the alchemical operation from the four grosser elements.
Yet Hermetic writers are agreed that this Quintessence is
really the root or source of the four elements Fire, Water,
Air, and Earth.

Their teaching exactly parallels that of the Yogis, who
call the five classes of expression the five *Tattvas*. These
are: Akasha (Quintessence); Tejas or Agni (Fire); Apas
(Water); Vayu (Air); Prithivi (Earth). Furthermore the Yogi
philosophy definitely states that the five tattvas are the
subtle principles of sensation; that each Tattva has its own
peculiar property; and that there is a cyclic ebb and flow
of the Tattvas, in regular sequence, through all things and
creatures.

One of the most important Yogic practices aims at control of this cyclic flow of the Tattvas. Similarly, in alchemy,
we hear of the Wheel of the Elements, with the Quintessence at the center. It is illustrated in Key 10 of the Tarot.
Concerning it Ripley writes: "But first of these elements
make thou rotation, and into Water thy Earth turn first of
all; then of thy Water make Air by levigation; and Air make
Fire; then Master will I thee call of all our secrets great
and small: The Wheel of Elements thou canst turn about,
Truly conceiving our writings without doubt." (*Compound
of Alchymie*, Sec. I: 17)

The preparation for the practice of yoga is the same in
all essentials as the preparation for the practice of alchemy.
Evil tendencies are to be overcome, and positive virtues
developed. The gross functions of the body are to be purified, and then comes the finer purification of the interior
centers. The object of all these yoga practices is precisely
that which is mentioned by Basil Valentine, namely, that
the yogi's body "may be transmuted into a holy temple of
God and purged from all uncleanness."

Again, the fire of alchemy is said to be a secret fire,

which is often compared to a serpent or dragon. Likewise in yoga, the active principle of the operation is a fiery force coiled in the Saturn center at the base of the spine. It is known as *Kundalini*, the coiled serpent power.

The aim of all yoga practice is to raise this serpent power, stage by stage, through the seven chakras which we have identified with the alchemical metals. Thus the practice of yoga is really a process of sublimation, which lifts up and brings into active manifestation the hidden powers of the subconscious life of man. In other words, yoga calls forth the powers of the Osirian "underworld." In alchemy we have exactly the same kind of practice.

Finally, Paracelsus, like the rest of the sages, tells his readers that the Great Work is performed by the aid of Mercury, and that the only other agencies entering into the art are the powers of the Sun and Moon. In like manner, the yoga system recognizes two agencies. One, hot and fiery, is called *Prana* or *Surya* (Sun). The other, cold and moist, is named Rayi, and is always termed the lunar current.

Let us conclude, then, by resuming these parallels in a table:

Yoga Philosophy		Alchemy	
All things are expressions of one fundamental energy.		All things are from one, by the mediation of one.	
All things combine three qualities:		All things combine three principles:	
SATTVA	Wisdom	MERCURY	Wisdom
RAJAS	Desire-force	SULFUR	Desire-force
TAMAS	Inertia	SALT	Inertia
There are five modes of expression:		There are five modes of expression:	

YOGA PHILOSOPHY	ALCHEMY
AKASHA	QUINTESSENCE
TEJAS	FIRE
APAS	WATER
VAYU	AIR
PRITHIVI	EARTH
There are seven principal vehicles of action, called lotuses or chakras:	There are seven principal substances to be transmuted, termed metals or planets:
MULADHARA Base of Spine	SATURN Lead
SVADISTTHANA Naval	MARS Iron
NANIPURA Solar Plexus	JUPITER Tin
ANAHATA Cardiac Plexus	SOL Gold
VISUDDHI Throat Center	VENUS Copper
AJNA Pituitary Body	LUNA Silver
SAHASRARA Pineal Gland	MERCURY Quicksilver
There is a secret force, fiery in quality, which is to be raised from the lower chakras to the higher ones.	The lower metals, or their essences, are to be raised into the forms and essences of higher ones by sublimation.
The Sun (Prana), Moon (Rayi), and Sattva (Wisdom) are the three main agencies of the work of the Yogis.	All the alchemists agree that the Great Work is performed through the power of the Sun and Moon, aided by Mercury.

Both alchemy and yoga aim at the illumination of the operator, at the transformation of his physical body, and at control of the subtle forces of nature.

Summing up this lesson, then, we may say that the basis of alchemy is the doctrine that man is the direct expression of the perfectly free, unmodified spiritual essence of all things. The alchemical work is the direction of the energy derived from that essence, according to the perceptions of awakened intelligence. This intelligence, the self-conscious mind of man, though it is not the highest level of life expression, has this power: It can perceive the order of nature, by discerning the principles behind the veil of appearances. Furthermore, in its ability to discover principles, and in its power of control over the subconscious life of the human body, it combines the two greatest potencies known to us. For by the recognition of the principles upon which the body is built, and its environment brought into form, the intelligence of man is able to invent and carry into execution novel applications of those principles. Thus it is possible to bring about a finer adjustment, and a finer organization, of the human body itself.

The result of so doing is the production of a new kind of human being, capable of receiving the influx of forms of energy which would disintegrate the ordinary human body, and able to give expression to modes of consciousness which are not characteristic of the great number of men and women.

The alchemist himself is the subject of the primary stages of his operation. The laboratory in which he works is his own personality. His practice enables him to demonstrate that his personality is the field of the Operation of the Sun. Step by step it gradually and gently alters the state of his mind and of his body until he reaches a stage of illumination in which he perceives that all his personal activities are in truth particular modes of a cosmic process.

This understanding enables him to reverse the mental attitude taken by most persons. It also enables him to exercise powers undreamed of by the mass of humanity. In him is fulfilled the saying of Eliphas Levi: "He who can master and direct the currents of the Astral Light may reduce the world to a chaos and transform its face."

As the alchemist completes the Great Work, he comes

to realize his inner identity with the One Power which is *always* dominant over all things, *always* the ruler of all forces, and *always* the determiner of the constitution of everything. At the end of the Great Work the alchemist has so transmuted his personality that he expresses nothing but the inwardly perceived impulses of that One Power in whatever he thinks, says, or does. As a free channel for the dominant principle of the universe, his personality expresses that dominion in works of power, and these works appear to be miracles when viewed by uninitiated beholders.

To this high goal we direct your aspiration. It may seem far beyond you now, yet the wisdom of the ages is agreed that whosoever will persist in the Great Work, carrying it out perseveringly, stage by stage, will undoubtedly be able to complete it.

In this New Age what has been known to the adepts of other generations may be told more openly than ever before. It may not *all* be told, because some of it is actually untellable. But here you will find no false leads, no willful distortions of the doctrine, no unnecessary concealments. Here is the essence of the Hermetic doctrine. Put it into practice, and you will certainly accomplish the Great Work.

II
THE FIRST MATTER

*T*hroughout the literature of Hermetic science there is perfect agreement among the adepts as to one fundamental tenet: success in the Great Work depends upon what they call the "discovery" of the First Matter. Right here we must be alert. The meaning of words changes as the years pass, and we shall be led astray if we suppose that to "discover", in alchemical doctrine, is exactly the same as to "find." We must go back to the older meanings of the verb "discover," back to its derivation – even back to the Hebrew verb which is translated "discover" in the Authorized Version of the Old Testament.

Literally, to discover is to lay bare, to denude, to strip of concealment. This is the exact significance of the Hebrew verb גלה, *galah*, which we have just mentioned. One of the meanings of this verb in Hebrew is "to open a book," and in this connection the reader familiar with Tarot will notice that the first letter of the verb is Gimel, represented in the Tarot Keys by the High Priestess, who holds in her lap an open book or scroll. The second letter is Lamed, represented by Key Eleven, Justice, which has equilibrium for its fundamental meaning. The last letter is Heh, typified by the Emperor, symbol of reason and of dominion over the conditions of physical existence.

Furthermore, since the first letter of גלה is that which is associated with memory, it appears that in order to denude the First Matter of its veil of concealment, we must employ the power of recollection and association represented by the High Priestess. Indeed, the High Priestess herself is a symbol of the First Matter, as we shall see more clearly by the time we come to the end of this lesson. The

discovery of the Matter is not the term of a quest undertaken in the world about us. It is the unveiling of the true
nature of something within us, and it is accomplished in
very truth by an act of recollection.

Deep in our subconsciousness lies hidden the secret of
the First Matter. To bring it to the surface is the primary
object of Hermetic practice, just as it is the primary object of yoga. Thus the letter Lamed, among other things a
symbol of that true faith which takes form in persevering
action, enters into the composition of the verb נלה. Without faith in the actual existence of the First Matter, it will
never be discovered. If we share the world's opinion that
the alchemists were fools, we shall never participate in
their wisdom, for we shall never be able to persist through
the preliminary stages of the Great Work, sticking to our
practice day in and day out, through that period of testing
and trial in which no outward and visible signs of success
reward our efforts. For, as the final letter of נלה shows, the
discovery is to be made with the mind alone, even as we
learned from the Upanishad quoted in the first lesson. In
its initial stages it is a rational process.

We begin with the words of the sages. Over and over,
in their books, they tell us what the First Matter is. At
first what they say seems to be a meaningless mass of ver-
biage. Then, as we persist in bringing our attention again
and again to what they say, the inner significance begins
to show, like the outline of a figure covered by a drapery.
Then, by comparing the various descriptions, we are able
to reason out what the First Matter *must* be.

The actual discovery, however, is by no means merely
an inference. There is no guesswork about it. It is vivid,
unmistakable experience. When you have discovered the
First Matter, you *know* that you have done so. Nobody can
argue you out of that knowledge. It is not an opinion. It
is not simply what *you* think. You share the experience of

the sages. All that they **have written** on this topic becomes perfectly clear to you.

At the same time you **understand** why none of the adepts ever tells, in plain **language**, what the First Matter really is. You understand that **the** secret simply *cannot* be told, because it is a knowledge **for** which there are no adequate verbal expressions.

Perhaps you doubt this now. Perhaps you think that the ingenuity of man is equal to the task of finding a name for anything in his experience. True enough, but the point is that the name will convey no meaning to the person who has not also had the experience. Paracelsus and some others invented names for certain experiences that are familiar to every adept in the Hermetic practice. But how much do these names mean to their uninitiated readers? Less than nothing. Even to those who have made the discovery, these new terms are no better than the old ones. He who knows what the First Matter really is never has any difficulty with the obscure language of the sages.

Well, if all this be true, you may ask, what's the use of reading the alchemical writers? You say they cannot tell the secret. Why bother with their attempts to do so? The answer to this is that what they do say leads us to the point where we can infer what they mean. Then our inference can be tested by experimental work. If the inference is wrong, it leads to nothing. When it is correct, it leads to the actual discovery.

What we aim to do for you in these lessons is to put you in the way of making the correct inferences from the words of the sages. Then we propose indicating the methods whereby you may test those inferences for yourself. To this end we shall begin with a series of quotations from various alchemical texts. We have endeavored so to arrange these quotations that as you read them your mind may be led by the mere reading nearer to the truth. In addition to this careful arrangement of the material, we shall also give you a concise commentary which will assist you to arrive at your conclusions as to the real meaning.

Take your time about this. One of the reasons for our decision to make this a monthly course is that haste and impatience will but retard your progress. In separating the ethereal spirit from the gross letter of the quotations, remember the admonition of the *Emerald Tablet*, and perform the operation with sweetness as well as with ingenuity. Bear ever in mind the truth that the real object of the Hermetic practice is identical with the real object of yoga. That object is nothing less than the complete liberation of the alchemist from the bondage of delusion.

It is by no means an utter abandonment of the world, as many have supposed. As one Eastern writer puts it: "The knower of the Essence, enjoying the pleasures of the senses with moderation, *but knowing them for what they are*, may derive both temporal and spiritual pleasure, even like one having knowledge of two languages." (*Panchadasi*). And what is it to know the enjoyments that come through the various channels of sensation for what they are? This is the answer given in the *Yogavasishtha*: "The whole world is Spirit, there is no thing else in reality; Betake thyself to this view of things, and rest in peace, thus regaining thy real self."

So much by way of introduction. Read the following quotations slowly and carefully. At first, let your main object be to grasp what they say. The adepts write carefully, and choose their words with great pains. Your first endeavor should be to impress those words upon your memory, without making any effort whatever towards interpretation. The less you try to guess what these declarations mean, the quicker will the correct interpretation dawn upon you.

The original matter is really a kind of stone, which being hard and solid like a stone, may be pounded, reduced to powder, and resolved into its three elements (which Nature herself has joined together), and then again may be recombined into a solid stone of the fusibility of wax, by the skilled hand of the artist, adjusting the law of Nature. (*The Sophic Hydrolith*)

The Sages have, indeed, purposely concealed their meaning under a veil of obscure words, but it is sufficiently clear from their writings that the substance of which they speak is not of a special, but a general kind, and is therefore contained in animals, vegetables, and minerals. It would, however, be unwise to take a roundabout road where there is a shorter cut; and they say that whereas the substance can be found in the animal and vegetable kingdoms only with great difficulty, and at the cost of enormous labor, in the bowels of the earth it lies ready to our hands. It is the matter which the Sages have agreed to call Mercury or Quicksilver. Our quicksilver, indeed, is truly a living substance, so called not because it is extracted from cinnabar, but because it is derived from the metals themselves. (Edward Kelly, *The Humid Path*)

(N.B. This quotation from Kelly needs to be read with special care, because it is apparently so open and matter-of-fact. The key to it, which should unlock the mystery for students of Tarot, is the phrase, "in the bowels of the earth it lies ready to our hands." Observe, too, that Kelly says the sages have agreed to call this matter Mercury, and that he specifically declares that "our" quicksilver is not extracted from cinnabar, the ordinary mercurial ore of the mines.)

The matter of our Stone, Mercury, is a commonly diffused subject, and though it is found with greater ease in some minerals, it may be discovered everywhere. In this sense

Morienus, that illustrious Sage, answered King Calid's question as to the matter of the Stone in the following way: 'It is of thee, O King, and thou art its ore.' And Raymond asserted that he had extracted his substance from a vile and worthless thing. (– *Ibid.*)

The First Matter is often called Magnesia, and is thus described in the glossary to A.E. Waite's translation of the *Hermetic and Alchemical Writings of Paracelsus*:

MAGNESIA. This term, which is occasionally used by Paracelsus in its alchemical, as distinct from its chemical sense, has received many explanations from the adepts. It is the matter of the stone, which the philosophers sometimes call their red, and sometimes their white magnesia. In the first preparation the chaos is blood-red, because the central sulfur is stirred up and discovered by the philosophical fire. In the second it is exceedingly white and transparent like the heavens. It is something like common quicksilver, but of such a celestial and transcendent brightness, that nothing on earth can be compared to it. It is a child of the elements, a pure virgin, from whom nothing has been generated as yet. When she breeds, it is by the fire of Nature, which is her husband. She is neither animal, vegetable, nor mineral, nor is she an extraction from these; she is pre-existent to them all, and is their mother. She is a pure simple substance, yielding to nothing but love, because generation is her aim, and that is never accomplished by violence. She produces from her heart a thing, heavy, snow-white water, which is the *Lac Virginis* (Virgins Milk), and afterwards blood from her heart. Lastly she presents a secret crystal. She is one and three, but at the same time she is four and five. She is the Catholic Magnesia, the Sperm of the World, out of which all natural things are generated. Her body is in a sense incorruptible; the common elements will not destroy it, neither does she mix with them essentially. Outwardly she resembles a stone, and yet she is no stone. The philosophers call her their white gum, water of their sea, water of life, most pure and blessed water; she is a thick, permanent, saltish water, which does not wet the hand, a dry water, viscous and slimy, and generated from the saline fatness of the earth. Fire cannot destroy her, for she is herself fire, having within her a portion of the universal fire of Nature, and a secret, celestial spirit, animated and quickened by God. She is a middle nature, between thick and thin, not altogether earthly, not wholly igneous, but a mean normal substance, to be found everywhere and at all seasons. (*Hermetic and Alchemical Writings of Paracelsus*)

As concerns the matter, it is *one*, and contains within itself all that is needed. Its birth is in the sand. It is the distilled moisture of the Moon joined to the light of the Sun and congealed. (Anastratus, *The Crowd*)

Know that our Mercury is before the eyes of all men, though it is known to few. When it is prepared its splendor is most admirable; but the sight of it is vouchsafed to none, save the sons of knowledge. Do not despise it, therefore, when you see it in sordid guise; for if you do, you will never accomplish our Magistery- and if you can change its countenance, the transformation will be glorious. For our water is a most pure virgin, and is loved of many, but meets all her wooers in foul garments, in order that she may be able to distinguish the worthy from the unworthy. Our beautiful Maiden abounds in inward graces; unlike the immodest woman who meets her lovers in splendid garments. To those who do not despise her foul exterior, she then appears in all her beauty, and brings them an infinite dower of riches and health. (*Philalethes*)

Basil Valentine writes: "Cease to seek it in the animal kingdom; for Nature herself could not find it there." He also says it is a mineral, and incombustible. It cannot be found in the animal kingdom because there its real nature is too completely veiled. It is incombustible because no fire can burn the essence of fire. It is mineral, because it is actually the real substance of whatever is to be found in mines.

It is a stone and no stone, Spirit, Soul and Body; which if thou dissolvest, it will be dissolved, and if thou dost coagulate it, it will be coagulated, and if thou dost make it fly, it will fly, for it is volatile, or flying, and clear as a tear; afterwards it is made citrine, then saltish, but without shoots or crystals, and no men may touch it with his tongue. Behold, I have described it truly to thee, but I have not named it! Now, I will name it, and I say that if thou sayest it is Water, thou dost say the truth, and if thou sayest it is not Water, thou dost lie. Be not, therefore, deceived with manifold descriptions and operations, for it is by one thing, to which nothing extraneous may be added. (Arnoldus de Villa Nova)

This Mercury of the Wisemen is a watery element, cold and moist. This is their permanent water, the spirit of the body, the unctuous vapor, the blessed water, the virtuous water, the water of the Wisemen, the philosopher's vinegar, the mineral water, the dew of heavenly grace, the virgins milk, the bodily mercury, and with other numberless names it is named in the books of the philosophers, which names, though they are divers, notwithstanding, always signify one and the same thing, namely, the Mercury of the Wisemen. (Albertus Magnus)

The object of your desire is the one thing out of which all things are made. (Rosinus)

The matter itself is found everywhere. It flies with fowls in the air, swims with fishes in the sea, it is discerned by the reason of angels, and it governs man and woman. (George Ripley)

The matter lies before the eyes of all; everybody sees it, touches it, loves it, but knows it not. It is glorious and vile, precious and of small account, and is found everywhere. …but, to be brief, our Matter has as many names as there are things in this world; that is why the foolish know it not. (The Golden Tract)

It is set up for the ruin of many and the salvation of some. To the crowd this matter is vile, exceedingly contemptible and odious, but to the philosophers it is more precious than gems or gold. It loves all, yet it is well-nigh an enemy of all; it is to be found everywhere, yet scarcely any one has discovered it. (*A Rosicrucian Treatise*)

The 'dew of heaven' and the 'oiliness of the earth' are the materials for our work. It is therefore neither a mineral nor a metal. The Pythagorean 'Y' indicates that there are two mercurial substances in one root, Fire and Water – Ischamaim- namely 'Y', extracted from the substance in which all metals are contained. It is a salt dew of heaven, but a metallic dew, containing all colors. This dew can be coagulated by the Hermetic Art, and produces a sweet salt, or Manna. Its father is the Sun, its mother is the Moon, and from these two it receives its life, light, and brightness. From the Sun it receives its Fire, and from the Moon its light.

We find this dew in a coagulated state, and also dissolved. It falls into the depths of the earth, and its substance is the most subtle and ethereal part of the earth. From above comes its soul and spirit, Fire and Light, and enters the body of Salt. Thus it receives the power of all things from above and from below.

This mineral dew appears in all its colors of white, yellow, green, red and black. It appears corporeal to the external eye, but to the miners in the mountains it appears sometimes thick, watery, and dripping. The best dew is the one which is coagulated like an Electrum, or like transparent amber.

This heavenly dew and its power is contained in everything. It is treated by the world with contempt and rejected by it. As it grows, it becomes divided into two branches, white and red, both springing from one root – 'Y'. This substance grows out of that one root, appearing like a white and red rose of Jericho, and blooming like a lily in the Valley of Jehoshaphat.

It is often prematurely broken by the miners, and tortured by the ignorant workmen. But the true artist observes its influence by his developed internal senses, and gathers it when it is ripe, with its flowers, seeds, root, trunk, and branches.

Let these hints be sufficient! It is neither a metal nor a mineral, but the mother of all metals and minerals, and their Prima Materia. It is nothing else but the coagulated blood of the Red Lion, and the Gluten of the Eagle. IF YOU DISCOVER IT, BE SILENT AND KEEP IT SACRED. (*The Secret Symbols of the Rosicrucians*)

Our Mercury is not common Mercury or quicksilver; but our Mercury is a water which cannot be found upon earth, for it is not made or manifested in the ordinary course of Nature, but by the art and manual operations of man. (Raymond Lully)

The seed of all things has been placed by God in water. This seed some exhibit openly, like vegetables, some keep in their kidneys, like animals, some conceal in the depths of their essential being, like minerals. The seed is stirred into action by a certain celestial influence, coagulates the material water, and passes through a series of fermentive processes (fermentation being the principle of all transmutation), until it has produced that for the production of which it was especially suited. (Philalethes)

This mystery, because of the malice and wickedness of men, is given only to few; notwithstanding it lives and moves everyday in the sight of the whole world, as it appears by the following parable: I am a poisonous dragon, present everywhere, and to be had for nothing. My water and my fire dissolve and compound; out of my body thou shalt draw the Green, and the Red Lion; but if thou dost not exactly know me, thou wilt with my fire destroy thy five senses. A most pernicious quick poison comes out of my nostrils, which hath been the destruction of many. Separate therefore the thick from the thin artificially, unless thou dost delight in extreme poverty. I give thee faculties both male and female, and the powers both of heaven and earth. The mysteries of my art are to be performed magnanimously, and with great courage, if thou wouldst have me overcome the violence of the fire, in which attempt many have lost both their labor and their substance. I am the Egg of Nature, known only to the Wise, such as are pious and modest, who make of me a little world. Ordained I was by the Almighty God for men; but though many desire me, I am given only to few, that they may relieve the poor with my treasures, and not set their minds on gold that perisheth. I am called of the philosophers Mercury; my husband is Gold philosophical. I am the old dragon that is present everywhere on the face of the earth; I am father and mother; youthful and ancient; weak and yet most strong; life and death; visible and invisible; hard and soft; descending to the earth, and ascending to the heavens; most high and most low; light and heavy; in me the order of Nature is oftentimes inverted, in color, number, weights and measure. I have in me the light of nature; I am dark and bright; I spring from the earth, and I come out of heaven; I am well known, and yet a mere nothing; all colours shine in me, and all metals by the beams of the sun. I am the Carbuncle of the Sun, a most noble clarified earth, by which thou mayest turn copper, iron, tin, and lead into most pure gold. (Quoted in Vaughen's *Coelum Terra* from a Rosicrucian original)

There exists a force in nature which is far more powerful than steam, by means of which a single man, who can master it and knows how to direct it, might throw the world into confusion and transform its face. It is diffused throughout infinity; it is the substance of heaven and earth; for it is either fixed or volatile according to its degrees of polarization. When it produces radiance it is called light. It is that substance which was created by God before all else when he said: Let there be light. It is substance and motion at one and the same time; it is a fluid and a perpetual vibration. The inherent force by which it is put into activity is called magnetism. In infinite space it is ether, or etherized light; it becomes astral light in the stars which it magnetizes, while in organized beings it becomes the magnetic light or fluid. In man it forms the astral body or plastic mediator. The will of intelligent beings acts directly on this light, and, by means thereof, upon all nature, which is made subject to the modifications of intelligence.

This agent is precisely what the medieval adepts called the first matter of the Great Work. This Universal Agent, this vital and luminous caloric, this electro-magnetic ether, is represented on ancient monuments by the girdle of Isis, which twines in a love-knot round two poles, by the bull-headed serpent, by the serpent with the head of a goat or a dog, and by the serpent devouring its own tail. It is the winged dragon of Medea, the double serpent of the caduceus, and the tempter of Genesis; but it is also the brazen snake of Moses, encircling the Tau; it is the Hyle of the Gnostics; and lastly, it is the devil of exoteric dogmatism, and is really the blind force which souls must conquer, in order to detach themselves from the chains of earth. (Eliphas Levi; *Mysteries of Magic*)

Very likely, after your first reading of the foregoing quotations, you will feel more bewildered than enlightened. In time, however, as you go over these words of the sages again and again, the inner meaning will begin to open itself to you. It would do so without any commentary, if you persisted long enough. In this day, however, there is particular need for the performance of the Great Work by just as many as may be made ready to undertake it. Thus what you would have had to learn by the slow method of repeated contemplation of the words of the adepts may now, in some measure at least, be made easier to grasp by means of commentary.

Let it be clearly understood, however, that it is just as impossible for us to discover the First Matter for you as it ever was. What we can and will do is to make it easier for you to draw the inferences which will prepare you to make that discovery. Be on your guard. As you proceed with this lesson, you may come to a point where you will say, "Why, of course! The First Matter is neither more nor less than..." whatever you may decide. You may conclude that it is identical with the ether of space. Or you may suppose it to be the same as what Hindus term *Akasha*. Mind, we are not saying that if you arrive at either of these conclusions you will be mistaken. What we are warning you against is the supposition that such a conclusion is the *discovery* of the First Matter.

Suppose you were at the entrance to an unlighted room, and you were hungry. Suppose you found on the door a cryptic description of the contents of the room, from which you drew the perfectly correct inference that on a table within you might find all manner of excellent food supplies. Could you satisfy your hunger with that inference?

So it is with the First Matter. Reason will show you what it must be, and we shall do all we can to assist you to use your reasoning powers to that end. We may even be able to turn on the light for you. But only you can find and use the things required to perform the Great Work.

First of all we shall call on Paracelsus for an important piece of information, commonly neglected by those who try to interpret alchemical writings. He says, in his *Tincture of the Philosophers*: "Now, if you do not understand the use of the Cabalists and the old astronomers, you are not born by God for the Spagyric art, or chosen by Nature for the work of Vulcan, or created to open your mouth concerning alchemical arts." He said this because he knows that the methods of the Qabalah, and the underlying ideas of astrology, are the keys to the meaning of the alchemical cryptic language. The first use we shall make of his hint to apply the Qabalah to the elucidation of our first quotation from the sages.

There we read that the original matter is really a kind of *stone*, which may be reduced to powder, and resolved into its three elements. Remembering that many alchemi-

cal terms are derived from Hebrew, we look up the word
for stone in that language, and find that it is composed of
three elements, or letters: Aleph, Beth, and Nun, which
form the word אבן, *Ehben*. The first letter, Aleph, according to Qabalists, represents *Ruach*, the Life Breath,
or Pure Spirit. The second represents Mercury. The third
represents the zodiacal sign Scorpio, symbolized sometimes by the Eagle, which typifies the reproductive power
in all living things, the principle of growth which is always
associated in ancient occult writings with water.

Thus we find that in the Hebrew word for *stone* there
are definitely indicated three characteristics which are
often mentioned in alchemical descriptions of the First
Matter. It is a vital essence (Aleph). It is something that
the adepts have agreed to call Mercury (Beth). It is something which they also designate as the Sperm or Seed of
the World, which they as often call Water, and which they
likewise term the Gluten of the Eagle (Nun).

This is only a beginning. The word אבן, *Ehben*, is peculiar in that its first two letters form the noun אב, meaning "Father", while the last two spell בן, *Ben*, meaning
"Son". Thus the First Matter is indicated as being something in which the Qabalistic ideas represented by these
two words are conjoined. Ab, Father, is a special name
given by Qabalists to that aspect of the Life Power which
they name Chokmah, or WISDOM. בן, Son, is one of their
names for that aspect of the same power which is termed
Tiphereth, BEAUTY.

In Qabalistic psychology, Chokmah or Wisdom is held
to be the seat of the life force in man, while Tiphereth, or
Beauty, is regarded as the seat of imagination. Thus the
word אבן intimates that the First Matter is really identical with the life force, and that it is also the power which
expresses itself in our lives as the active principle in the

production of mental imagery.

Here is the most important suggestion. For it is in full accord with the practical side of the yoga teaching. The latter is founded upon the idea that whatsoever exists is an expression of a conscious, vital energy which produces all the multiplicity of forms, on every plane, by precisely the same power that we exercise in the making of mental images. Patanjali tells us that Yoga is the control of the thinking principle, and if this means anything it must mean that yoga is control of the power that takes form as mental imagery. For even the most abstract thinking requires imagery. To be sure, in such thinking the images of physical objects are replaced by symbols, as, for example, in mathematics. Yet the symbols are none the less images, and they are combined and arranged just as if they were actual objects.

It is also noteworthy that the numeral value of אבן is fifty-three, which is also the value of the noun חמה, *Khammaw*, which we have found to be a component part of the word *Alchemy*. As the word itself signifies "Sun", we might say, Qabalistically, "Our Stone and the Sun are One," and we should be less cryptic than many of the alchemical writers. In this connection, also, we may note that the first letter of חמה is Cheth, which corresponds to the sign Cancer, ruled by the Moon; that the second represents the element water; and that the third corresponds to the sign of Aries, in which the Sun is exalted, according to astrologers. Thus the Hebrew word for *Sun* contains Qabalistically the ideas of Moon and Water as well as that of Sun. Hence the alchemists, who are continually reminding us that the matter of the Great Work, the materials, and the result, are all comprised in the right knowledge and use of what they call Sun, Water, and Moon, may well have had what we have just explained in mind when they formulated their cryptic statements.

Before leaving the word אבן, we may also note that the first part of the word (אב, Father) may be taken as a symbol of the universal Life-power, considered as the source, or parent, of all that exists. Similarly, the last half of the word (בן, the Son) is a symbol of Man, reproducing the essential characteristics of his heavenly parent. Needless to say that this should not be taken to mean what it does in ordinary theology. It is simply the idea that man is the offspring of the power which has brought the universe into existence, from which it follows that man shares in the fundamental nature of that power.

Passing now to Edward Kelly's remarks about the First Matter, let us point out more definitely what we had in mind in warning you not to take him too literally. Indeed, the opening words are a warning that no writing of the adepts is other than *intentionally* a veil that must be penetrated before the real meaning can be grasped. The cryptic portion of Kelly's writing, however, begins with the phrase, "in the bowels of the earth it lies ready to our hands." Kelly was a clever Qabalist and a first rate astrologer. He knew why alchemists call their First Matter *Lac Virginis*, or Virgin's Milk. He understood their reason for describing it as an unctuous, or oily, water. He accepted their doctrine that man is a microcosm. So he had no difficulty in compressing the essence of the alchemical doctrine into a phrase. Understand by "earth" the microcosm, man, and you will easily solve the puzzle. "The bowels of the earth" are the human intestinal tract, ruled by the earthly sign Virgo, the Virgin. The Virgin's Milk, the oily water which will not wet the hand, is actually chyle, the product of stomach digestion, which enters the intestines (the Black Dragon of Alchemy) in the form of a milky, fatty fluid, from which the lacteals in the small intestine absorb the various substances required for the replenishment of the blood stream.

Basically, those substances are organic forms of various minerals. Thus Kelly is essentially correct when he says that the First Matter is derived from the metals themselves, and when he insists that it is a living substance. He shows himself an ingenious Qabalist by declaring that in the bowels of the earth the First Matter is "ready to our hands." For in Qabalah the sign Virgo is attributed to the letter Yod, and the significance of the letter name יוד, *Yod*, is "hand." We shall see what another of our alchemical authors also refers to the letter Yod in connection with the First Matter.

As soon as we have identified the First matter with the contents of the intestinal tract, we can understand the answer given by Morienus to King Calid. We can also see why Raymond Lully, and many another, asserted that the substance might be extracted from something generally regarded as vile and worthless. We can understand why Philalethes, who also insists that the mysterious water is a *virgin*, declares that she meets her wooers in foul garments. And in the light of modern knowledge, which shows us that intestinal fermentation is one of the most fruitful sources of disease, we can understand the truth of the Rosicrucian declaration that the First Matter is set up for the ruin of many, and is well nigh an enemy of all.

Yet here again we must guard ourselves against the unwarranted assumptions that we have grasped the whole mystery when we have identified chyle as the *form* of the First Matter which is used in the alchemical process. Some readers of these pages, indeed, may doubt that anything so ordinary can possibly be the precious substance of the alchemists. Let them remember that Thomas Vaughan says that he knows most persons would regard the truth as laughable; and let them recall the story of Paracelsus, who promised to show the faculty of a university the Elixir of Life, and scandalized them all by uncovering a jar filled with excrement. Most of his contemporaries believed that he was guilty of a gross practical joke. The essence of the joke was that he actually kept his promise. For when the alchemical process is understood and carried out, the adept is able to extract from the chyle a great number of essences which are of inestimable value. These are wasted by the average human being because he does not know how to extract them. By gaining conscious control of the process of intestinal digestion and assimilation, the adepts in alchemy are enabled to fill their veins with the veritable elixir of life, the priceless liquid "gold" (Solar Energy) that not only maintains the vital functions indefinitely, but also makes possible the preparation of the true Stone of the Wise.

We repeat, nevertheless, that although what we have explained is a revelation of the alchemical mystery more definite than any other which has been given in the plain language of modern times, it is by no means the *discovery* of the First Matter. The quotation from Waite's glossary to Paracelsus (consisting largely of unacknowledgeable borrowings from Thomas Vaughan) makes this evident. Yet you will notice that even here there is mentioned the production of the Virgin's Milk, followed by that of blood-the same sequence that occurs in the body when chyle is taken up by the lacteals.

At the same time, even a slight acquaintance with the alchemical texts is enough to show that although the *form* of the First Matter employed in the alchemical operation is the Virgin's Milk, the Matter itself is not restricted to that form. It is therefore declared not to be an extraction from animal, vegetable, or mineral, but to be pre-existent to them all, and their mother. In this doctrine we have a close agreement with the Oriental idea of Prakriti, the root-substance from which all existing objects are differentiated.

Prakriti, which, in the seventh chapter of the *Bhagavad Gita*, is termed the "mysterious power, difficult to cross over," is identical with the Maya of the *S'vetasvatara Upanishad*, which declares: "Know nature to be Maya, and the Ruler of Maya as the Lord Himself."

Now, Maya is also the name of the mother of Hermes, so that from Greek mythology we get the hint that Maya is the root-principle which brings forth Mercury. It is not without significance, we think, that the mother of Buddha was also named Maya, for the illumination of Buddha is precisely the goal of the processes of alchemy and yoga.

Furthermore, there is a close connection between the words *Maya* and *Magia*, the latter being the Latin noun for *Magic*. In both words there is the dual conception of a power which manifests itself in changes and mutations, and of a power which is the cause of all human errors because its illusive nature, so long as it remains unrecognized, leads the mind of man into all sorts of mistaken judgments. Thus the alchemical texts tell us that the First Matter, in some of its aspects, is poisonous, and the enemy of all.

Jacob Boehme, himself steeped in alchemical literature, and blessed with that higher insight which leads to the actual discovery of the First Matter, employed the word Magic in the sense just explained. In the fifth chapter of his *Six Mystical Points* he writes:

> Magic is the mother of eternity, of the being of all beings; for it creates itself, and is understood in desire...It is the original state of nature. Its desire makes an imagination (Einbildung), and the imagination or figuration is only the will of desire...Magic is the formative power in the eternal wisdom. According as the will makes a model in wisdom, so does desiring Magic receive it; for it has in its property imagination as a longing. Imagination is gentle and soft, and resembles water.

Thus we see that Boehme perceived that the fundamental power which brings things into existence is like that which we know in ourselves as desire and imagination. Observe that he compares imagination to water, the commonest alchemical name for the First Matter. In his *Mysterium Pansophicum* he also says: "We recognize also from whence all things, evil and good, take their origin, namely from the Imagination in the great Mystery, where a wonderful essential life generates itself."

The term "Catholic Magnesia," mentioned on page 30, is often employed as a name for the First Matter. The adjective, "catholic," is to be understood as meaning "universal, infinite, and all pervading." As employed in alchemy, "magnesia" means *Magnes Lithos*, or lodestone, and thus refers to the magnetic power peculiar to that mineral. According to exoteric derivations, the magnet is named after the place, Magnesia, in Thessaly. Occultists are aware, however, that both "magnet" and "magic" are related to the Sanskrit terms *Mahat* and *Maya*. The Catholic Magnesia, or Universal Magnet, is the universal attractive principle which holds things together. It is therefore represented in Tarot by the High Priestess. For this attractive principle is a mode of consciousness, or intelligence. Therefore it is correctly symbolized by that Tarot Key which represents the Uniting Intelligence. Furthermore, the title of that Key, High Priestess, means " Chief Feminine Elder," and thus intimates what we have found to be a characteristic of alchemical and yoga descriptions of the *Prima Materia*. They all agree that the mysterious power is feminine in its quality, and again and again they use the pronoun "she" in referring to it.

Ordinary lodestone is a magnetic mineral which attracts iron, the metal of Mars. In mythology we read of a clandestine relationship between Mars and Venus. In your study of Tarot you learned that Venus is represented by the Empress, and that the Empress is really the High Priestess, become a mother by her association with the Magician. Thus you should have little difficulty in understanding what Thomas Vaughan means when he says the First Matter is a virgin substance, while in the same sentence he also declares it to be a "soft, prolific Venus, the very love and seed, the mixture and moisture of heaven and earth."

Of heaven, because the First Matter is "that which is above," and in that respect appears as the Tarot Magician, who represents the direction Above, and is a symbol also of what Eastern occultists call Purusha, the "superior nature" of the One Thing. So considered, the First Matter is called Mercury, as you will notice in the foregoing quotations. The First Matter is also of earth because it is likewise "that which is below," and then appears as the High Priestess, or virgin, who represents the direction Below, and is a symbol of the "inferior nature" of the One Thing, the Hindu Prakriti or Maya. In this aspect she is what the alchemists term their "Diana," and thus in Tarot the High Priestess wears the crescent, silver horns of the moon goddess. The Empress in Tarot represents the third aspect of the First Matter, as the prolific source of all sorts of forms, both good and evil. This is what Vaughan means when he calls the First Matter by the name Venus. Tarot students will also remember that the Empress represents imagination.

Do not relax your vigilance. It may seem to you that we have been sufficiently explicit. Have we not said that the First Matter is represented by the High Priestess and by the Empress, as well as by the Magician? Have we not told you that it is the power you employ daily in acts of desire and imagination? Is there anything more to know? Indeed there is! All this is no more than to tell you where to look, no more than to indicate to you the direction your research must take, before you may actually discover the

First Matter. What we have written will enable you to become well grounded in alchemical theory, but it must not be confused with practice. Be sure that you do not misunderstand us. Although we call the power which is expressed as imagination identical with the First Matter, such identification is not by any means the actual *perception* of that power.

When Eliphas Levi tells you there is a force more powerful than steam, by means of which you may reduce the world to confusion and transform its face, he is *not* delivering himself of mere hypothesis, despite the ignorant criticisms of his traducers. He speaks of that which he actually knows, of that which he has actually seen and felt, though the sight and touch are other than ordinary human sensations.

It is not surprising that Levi's principal accuser, A.E. Waite, whose notes on the French adept's writings are a source of combined annoyance and amusement to competent readers, should also declare that the alchemical doctrine of the First Matter is also no more than mere theory. This he does in a footnote on page 113 of the *Secret Tradition in Alchemy*, where he says: "It seems obvious that if the First Matter is everywhere and hence in all things it can be called by the names of all. But in reality its manifold denominations arise from the fact that the First Matter is hypothetical and is hence without a name."

This is simply not true. The First Matter is not at all hypothetical, except for persons like Mr. Waite, who, being for one reason or another unable to make the discovery, are thus brought to believe that want of experience of what the adepts write about is sufficient proof that there is nothing actually to experience. We can ourselves testify that the power which finds expression in desire and imagination is a real entity. We affirm, as the result of experience, that the force described by Eliphas Levi is by no means a mere theory. It is a force, and energy, a power, call it what you will, which is actually and really present, as the sages declare, "before the eyes of all, though seen by few."

The actual perception of this force is indispensable to success in the Great Work. For although we make use of the subtle powers of consciousness daily, though remaining ignorant of the force itself, true adeptship is founded on this actual perception. When the First Matter is, so to say, *seen and touched*, the first step toward adeptship is taken; and he who perseveres in the work until the end will be able, whenever a real need arises, to perform metallic transmutations on the physical plane. This without any metaphor whatever. He will be able, we repeat, but it is our opinion that he will seldom find occasion to exercise that particular power.

We trust that we have made our position clear. It does not greatly matter whether or not any one be convinced that we speak that which we know, and not that which is merely our opinion. Ours is a work of exposition, rather than of persuasion. As Ripley (not the alchemist) says: Believe it or not. Yet you can see how impossible it would be for one who considers the First Matter to be merely hypothetical ever really to discover it. As we said early in this lesson, they who make up their minds that there is no such thing prevent themselves from finding it.

They who reject the idea that the First Matter is an actual perceptible entity can never hope to know whether it is or not. On the other hand, if you accept too readily, you will probably be lacking in that eagerness for certainty which will carry you to the point where you can obtain it. The ideal state of mind in which to approach the Hermetic doctrine is one of moderate agnosticism, in the true sense of that abused word. If you say to yourself, "I do not *know* that the First Matter is a perceptible reality, neither do I *know* that it is not, but I intend to find out," you will be adopting the mental attitude most favorable to success in this kind of research.

We approach the conclusion of this lesson, but we have by no means completed our commentary on the words of the sages. This will be continued and completed in Lesson Three, and will include an extended commentary on the Rosicrucian document reproduced on page 33. we have already issued a short explanation of this text in the al-chemical section of the *First Year Extension Course* , but even if you have that, we believe you will find much that is of great interest in the next lesson.

During the coming month we advise you to familiarize yourself thoroughly with the various writings given in this lesson. Read and re-read them. Have at hand a note-book, for as you read you are likely to find ideas arising in your mind, some of which may be seed-thoughts that will later on prove to be very valuable. Our own experience has been that the study of the words of the sages puts one *en rap-port* with those members of the Inner School who have specialized in alchemy. We know very well that our own researches have been greatly aided from that source. The assistance often comes in the form of sudden inspirations or flashes of insight. These should be carefully recorded. The best way is to note them down as soon as they come. Otherwise the impression is apt to fade, sometimes be-yond recovery.

We cannot impress too strongly upon you the thought that in taking up the study of Hermetic science and prac-tice you are entering into an active circle of minds which includes various grades of adeptship. Every serious stu-dent of this subject attracts the attention of those who know more than himself, and if he shows ability and per-severance he will be helped.

The performance of the Great Work is no chimera, no

figment of the imagination. It is being carried on by numbers of sane, sensible human beings throughout the world. You are in some sense a candidate for admission to the company of those who have completed the Great Work. The more clearly you are assured of their actual presence among us, the more likely will you be to succeed in this undertaking.

On the other hand, what we have just said should not be construed to mean that more or less interest in alchemy, such as might lead to taking this course of lessons, or to the perusal of alchemical books, is enough to gain recognition from adepts of the Inner School. What is required is a degree of earnestness by no means common in this era of superficial dabbling in things occult.

We counsel you to a serious consideration of your aims in undertaking this study. Think well what it means. To succeed in the Great Work is no small thing. If such success be possible - and we find all the sages perfectly agreed that it is - what can be more important? What other concerns of your life can possibly take precedence over it? What else, of all that interests you, can be so thoroughly worth all the time and effort spent upon it?

Since it is the Occidental form of yoga, alchemy leads to precisely the same result as do the Oriental systems. That result is thus described by Vivekananda:

> When the Yogi becomes perfect there will be nothing in nature not under his control. If he orders the Gods to come, they will come at his bidding; if he asks the departed to come, they will come at his bidding. All the forces of nature will obey him as his slaves, and when the ignorant see these powers of the Yogi they call them miracles. (*Raja Yoga*, p31)

It is to no less a goal than this that the Great Work is directed. May you persist in it unto the end, which is the realization of perfect mastery, the demonstration of freedom from every kind of bondage.

III
THE FIRST MATTER II

On page 30 of the preceding lesson you will find the statement *"She is one and three, but at the same time she is four and five."* In this one sentence are several clues to the arcana of Hermetic science.

The First Matter is in itself a perfect unity. Hence the *Emerald Tablet* says: "All things are from one, by the meditation of one,...all things have their birth from this one thing by adaptation." And Kelly declares, "It is a commonly diffused subject." Similarly, Anastratus (quoted on page 31 of Lesson Two) says that the matter is one, and contains within itself all that is needed. The same declaration, with some variations of wording, is to be found in the writings of Rosinus, Ripley, and Eliphas Levi.

The First Matter is also three, because it contains within itself the three principles, sulfur, mercury, and salt. These are not three things of which the first matter is *composed*. It is not a composition, but a perfectly homogeneous unity. Rather are the three principles to be understood as being three aspects of the nature of the First Matter, inseparable from it and from each other.

Again, the First matter is said to be four because it is manifested in the form of the four elements, fire, water, air, and earth. These, as the *Book of Tokens* tells us, are really subtle or invisible entities, and should not be understood to signify anything which is limited to the physical plane. From the Yoga philosophy we learn that fire is the subtle principle of sight; that water is the subtle principle of taste; that air is the subtle principle of touch; and that earth is the subtle principle of smell. Each principle has also a characteristic property. The property of fire is expansion; that of water is contraction; that of air is locomotion;

and that of earth is cohesion. Each principle has also a characteristic taste-quality. Fire is hot; water is astringent, or bitter; air is acid or sour and sharp; earth is sweet. These last should be compared with what Jacob Boehme has to say about a twofold fire, and about bitterness and sharpness. Boehme knew nothing of Yoga philosophy as such, but he had had the same kind of experience which results from Yoga practice, and the same kind of insight. It is very significant, therefore, that he used alchemical language in all his attempts to explain what he had experienced.

The subtle principles of the Yoga philosophy are sometimes called *ethers*, as in Rama Prasad's book, *Nature's Finer Forces*, where we read that tejas (fire) is the luminiferous ether; that apas (water) is the gustiferous ether; that vayu (air) is the tangiferous ether; and that prithivi (earth) is the odoriferous ether.

We do not like this confusing use of the word "ether." In the esoteric teaching, there are said to be subdivisions of the ether, and these are sometimes loosely designated as the first, second, third, and fourth ethers; but the term properly belongs only to what H.P.B. rightly calls the grossest manifestation of Akasha, and Akasha, as shown in Lesson One, is identical with the alchemical quintessence.

The Hindu name for "principle" is *Tatva*, sometimes spelled *Tattwa*. Its literal meaning is "reality." This meaning carries a genuine significance. It indicates that the Tatvas are not merely hypothetical entities. They have actual being. They are not just human notions or names. They are real forces which give us our consciousness of sight, and taste, and touch, and smell. From these, and from the fifth principle, out of which they all proceed or are derived, we formulate our whole consciousness of the world around us. We perceive nothing whatever directly. All that we are aware of is the combination of sensations. Not that what we perceive in the world around us is not real. But the reality is not the same as our sensory perceptions. *Our* world is a synthesis of sensations. The real world cannot be known directly by sensation.

The First Matter is five, because it also includes another principle besides the four whose activities produce in us the ordinary experience of a physical world. In alchemical writings this principle is called the quintessence, and is usually said to be "extracted" from the four elements in the course of the Great Work. This is said because we derive our awareness of the fifth principle from our experience of the operation of the other four. The quintessence, however, is not in itself an extraction from the four other principles. It is not derived from them. They are derived from it.

The Hindu term is Akasha. Akasha is said to have neither touch, taste, color, nor odor. Its fundamental quality is that of space. But here we encounter a difficulty. There is a difference between absolute space, or Akasha, and relative space, such as we ordinarily conceive. The relative space, as Einstein has indicated, is curved and finite. It may not be very exact to say that Akasha, or absolute space, *contains* relative space, but this is as near as we can come to the truth of the matter, considering the limitations of human speech.

Akasha, moreover, is the subtle principle of sound. It is not the ordinary sound which is carried in waves through the air. It is the original power of vibration. It is the undifferentiated Life-power, the source of all other manifestations of every kind. For this unmanifest reality we can frame no adequate definition. To us it seems to be nothing, or we find ourselves thinking of it as being perfectly empty space. This is why the sages of India declare that space is the fundamental quality of Akasha. Because space is omnipresent, they also teach that Akasha is all pervading.

Rama Prasad says: "The Akasha is the most important of all the Tattvas. It must, as a matter of course, precede and follow every change of state on every plane of life. Without this there can be no manifestation or cessation of forms. *It is out of Akasha that every form comes, and it is in Akasha that every form lives.* The Akasha is full of forms in their potential state. It intervenes between every two of the five Tattvas." Here, by the way, is a hint for Tarot students as to the place of the Fool in the whole series. In the pack of cards, the Fool, comes before the number 1. The power he represents, however, is that which precedes every number, and follows every one. Between every number there is the zero, so that what is understood in the series, 1, 2, 3, 4, etc., is really 0, 1, (0), 2, (0), 3, etc. It is also noteworthy that the zero-sign, an oval, is also the Hindu symbol for Akasha.

Many symbols refer to the idea that the First Matter is *"one, which is also three, four, and five."* Among them is the Great Pyramid, ONE Structure, representing the number THREE by its triangular faces, the number FOUR by its square base, and the number FIVE by its apex and four corners. The apron worn by Free Masons (which, when properly proportioned, contains the fundamental pyramid measures) is also a unity, representing the number THREE by its triangular flap, the number FOUR by the square shape of the apron itself, and the number FIVE by the five corners of the apron and flap combined. Yet another familiar symbol of the First Matter is the celebrated Pythagorean triangle, sacred to Osiris, Isis, and Horus, having these proportions:

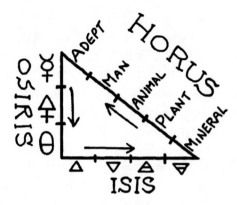

In this triangle the figure itself is the ONE representing the all-pervading First Matter. The descending vertical line of Osiris, the Father, is attributed to the THREE Principles, Mercury ☿, Sulfur 🜍, and Salt ⊖. The horizontal line, attributed to Isis, the Mother, has four units, representing the FOUR: Fire △, Water ▽, Air 🜁, and Earth ▽. The ascending line, containing FIVE units, and representing Horus, the son of Isis and Osiris, shows the five stages in the development of the Life-power's manifestation. The first stage is that of the mineral. Then comes the plant. After the plant is the animal. Above the animal is the natural man. Above the natural man is the man who has made himself the subject of the Great Work, the man who is adept, master, and magus, the man who completes the Great Work by becoming one with the Father, even as the line of Horus in this triangle completes itself by arriving at the point whence the lines of Osiris descends.

You will remember that in the preceding lesson (pages 38 to 40) we discussed the esoteric meaning of the word אבן, *Ehben*, and found that it combines the words אב, *Ab*, Father, and בן, *Ben*, Son. We also noticed that the value of the word is fifty-three, and that this is likewise the value of חמה, *Khammaw*, poetical Hebrew for "Sun." We have just seen that the descending line of the Pythagorean triangle is ascribed to Osiris, and the ascending hypotenuse to Horus. Osiris is the Father, and Horus is the Son. Thus Osiris is אב, and Horus is בן. Both, too, are solar deities. Hence it is interesting to find that the angle formed by the junction of the hypotenuse, or line of the Son, with the vertical line, or line of the Father, is an angle of fifty-three degrees. This, of course, makes the other angle of the triangle, at the point where the hypotenuse springs upward from the base, or from Isis the Mother, an angle of thirty-seven degrees.

The angular relation of the hypotenuse to the base is always that of thirty-seven degrees, and the angular relation of the same line to the line of Osiris is always fifty-three degrees, at any given point on the hypotenuse. The relation of the evolving forms of the Life-power to Mother Nature is always the same. The same laws and forces are at work in the stone as in the adept or master. Only the degree of expression is higher in the master than in the mineral. In the stone the direction or impulse of those laws and forces is also the same as it is in the master. All the forces of nature move together toward the perfect union of the Son with the Father, and toward the perfect union, also, of the powers of the Father and the Mother in the manifestation of the Son.

But we must not give too much space to this triangle. It deserves, and will have, a special essay, for all its wonders cannot be compressed into a few paragraphs, or even a few pages. The main point, however, should be clear. The Pythagorean triangle is a summary of the fundamentals of alchemy, showing the descent of Spirit into Nature as the cause of the ascent of consciousness through five great stages, back to perfect identification with the Primal Source.

It may be well, however, to say that we are by no means advancing the opinion that the ancient Egyptians had alchemy in mind when they adopted the Pythagorean triangle as a symbol of their Holy Family. All that we affirm is that there is evidence that this triangle has been used by alchemists to summarize their doctrine, because its mathematical properties are such that it lends itself easily to that purpose.

There are occasional references to this triangle in alchemical books. Again, several esoteric societies have made the alchemical meanings which we have briefly summarized an important part of the occult instruction imparted to their members.

There is abundant evidence that the Pythagorean triangle is a key to much in Rosicrucian symbolism. It is itself a prominent Masonic symbol, and is also clearly related to the most important of Masonic emblems, the white lambskin apron. Besides this, one finds references to it in many ancient rituals of organized Western occultism, always in connection with Hermetic doctrines.

The main point, however, is that its lines and angles do really constitute a remarkable summary of the main points of Hermetic science. We have received our knowledge concerning this fact through the channel of oral tradition, but the fact would still remain if the writers of these pages had been the first to notice it.

When Anastratus, in *The Crowd*, says of the First Matter, "*Its birth is in the sand*," he is referring to the mineral stage of development represented in the Pythagorean triangle. But to those who remember that one must apply Qabalistic principles to the interpretation of alchemical writings his words convey still more. In Hebrew "sand" is

חול, *khool*, derived from a verbal root meaning "to turn, to twist, to dance." Its significance in relation to sand is easily understood when one thinks how sand whirls and

dances as wind passes over it. The same noun also means:
1) a circle, reminding us of the esoteric idea that the circle is the fundamental form of manifestation; 2) a bird,
traditionally the phoenix, which is a familiar alchemical
term, signifying the fire in the quintessence, and also the
physical substance, stone. חול, moreover, is the root of
the Hebrew proper name *Havilah*, the land, according to
Genesis, "where there is gold."

The numeral value of חול, again, is forty-four, and this
is the value of the word דם, *Dam*, "blood," and of the name
of the eleventh zodiacal sign, דלי, *Dolee*, "Aquarius." Thus
we have a clear indication that the first manifestation of
the Matter is in the mineral kingdom, that it is also to be
found in blood, and that it has some connection with the
esoteric meanings of the zodiacal sign Aquarius. As man
uses it, the First Matter is actually a mineral substance,
circulating in the blood stream, and directly connected
with the functions of the heart, which is influenced, astrologers tell us, by the sign Aquarius, through reflex action. It might be still more accurate to say that the First
Matter is present as a mineral in the blood, in the form of
the twelve tissue salts (and then it would be apparent that
the twelve divisions of the Pythagorean triangle might also
refer to these twelve salts).

Like the phoenix, the First Matter is incombustible,
because its inner nature is the very essence of fire, and this
cannot be injured by fire. It is a whirling, circulating essence, that dances through our veins, moves more slowly
through the lymphatic vessels, and gyrates rapidly through
the entire nervous system. But the main point to bear in
mind is that it actually is ready for our use in its mineral
forms.

Let us now take up in detail the statements of the
Rosicrucian alchemical text quoted on page 33 in the pre-

ceding lesson. The first sentence of this quotation is an allusion to Genesis 27:28: "Therefore God give thee of the dew of heaven, and the fatness of the earth, and plenty of corn and wine."

DEW OF HEAVEN: In Hebrew this is טל השמים, *Tal Ha-Shamim*, and its number is four hundred and thirty-four. This is the number of דלת, *Daleth*, the Door, the Hebrew letter which is the sign of the Luminous Intelligence and of the planet Venus, associated with the center at the well of the throat. In this connection remember that more than one alchemist speaks of the First Matter as *Venus*.

The heavenly dew is light. It is identical with electricity. It is granular in structure, so that it actually falls like dew upon the earth, and the weight of its fall may be measured. In the 16th, 18th and 19th Tarot Keys this dew is shown falling in drops shaped like the letter י or "Y", and in some of the older esoteric versions of the cards, these drops are blood red, reminding us that there is a correspondence between חול, Sand, and דם, Dam, Blood.

THE OILINESS OF THE EARTH: In Hebrew this is הארץ שמני, *Shemeni Ha-Aretz*. Its number is six hundred and ninety-six. The digits of this add to twenty-one, and six hundred and ninety-six is itself the multiplication of the sum of numbers from 1 to 21 (231) by 3. Qabalistically, therefore, six hundred and ninety-six represents the threefold multiplication of the extension of the idea contained in the word אהיה, *Eheyeh*, Existence, the Divine Name attributed to the first aspect of the Life-power, the Primal Will. In other words, for any Qabalist, the number six hundred and ninety-six would represent the fullest possible development of actual existence.

The word "oil" in Hebrew is שמן. Its numeration is 390, also the number of ונקבהזכר, "male and female," of

שמים, "heaven", and of ספרים, *Sepharim*, "letters." The oil (שמן) is identical with the power of the heavens (ם שמי), is manifested on every plane as male and female זכר ונקבה), and is expressed by the vibratory and conscious forces represented by the twenty two letters (ספרים). In plain language, the *oiliness of the earth* is human flesh and blood, male and female, incarnating the invisible but real forces of the heavens, and expressing those forces through the twenty two modes of intelligence represented by the Keys of Tarot.

NEITHER MINERAL NOR METAL: This seems to contradict some of the other alchemical authorities, but the intention is to show that although the First Matter expresses as minerals and metals, it is not restricted to those forms. It is more than metal, more than mineral. Yet we must remember that because it is heavily veiled in the animal and vegetable forms of its manifestation, the discovery of the First Matter is most easily made by means of meditative contemplation of mineral forms, particularly crystals and stones which have been taken from the depths of the earth or from running water.

THE PYTHAGOREAN Y: In the original text from which we have quoted, the "Y" is shown as above. The left hand branch is surmounted by the alchemical symbol for sulfur, and the right hand branch by the symbol for mercury. Sulfur is a symbol for fire, and mercury, as a fluid metal, represents alchemical water. These are the "two mercurial substances in one root, fire and water." The "root" is said to be Y because Y is the Roman letter equivalent to Hebrew Yod, and Yod, as the letter which corresponds to the sign Virgo, represents that in us whence the material used in the Great Work is derived. According to ancient tradition, the letter "Y" was used by Pythagoras as a symbol of human life, with its two roads, the familiar "right-hand" and "left-hand" paths of occult development.

Isch Schamaim is one way of rendering a compound Hebrew word combining the nouns אֵשׁ, *Isch*, fire, and שָׁמַיִם, *Schamaim*, heaven. אֵשׁ שָׁמַיִם has a total numeration of 691. This is the value of the noun תְּרוּפָה, *teroofaw*, a remedy, a medicine. Notice that the digits of this word add to seven, thus hinting at the balanced operation of the seven alchemical metals in the Universal Medicine, or Elixir of Life. Seven is also the number of the letter Zayin, and the letter name זַיִן is the number sixty-seven, equivalent to בִּינָה, *Binah*, Understanding.

Now, in בִּינָה are combined the letters of יָהּ, *Jah*, the Father and בֵּן, *Ben*, the Son. בִּינָה is therefore similar in meaning to אַבָּן. What this means is that the adept's consciousness, in which the fire of heaven (אֵשׁ הַמַּיִם) is fully manifested, is a perfect union of the personal mind with the universal. This consciousness is correctly termed the Universal Medicine, because it is a mode of knowing which automatically establishes a condition of wholeness throughout the organism. Adepts have perfect bodily health because they are mentally at one with that which is the directive principle of all physical activity.

Y, EXTRACTED FROM THE SUBSTANCE IN WHICH ALL METALS ARE CONTAINED: Y, as we have said, is the letter Yod. In Qabalah it is also the symbol of the Intelligence of Will. It corresponds to the 9th Tarot Key, The Hermit. There you see the dew of heaven falling from a lantern, which contains as a light source the hexagram, or six pointed star, formed from the male, upright triangle of fire interlaced with the female, inverted triangle of water. The substance from which all metals are extracted is light. Y is said to be extracted from it because the most important work of alchemy has to do with the physiological functions in the part of the body ruled by Virgo. These functions extract the alchemical materials from the chyle, or Virgin's Milk, but the force extracted is light-force.

A SALT DEW OF HEAVEN, BUT A METALLIC DEW: A slight current of electricity has a saltish, and a metallic, taste. The heavenly dew is metallic because every metal is made from light. The text goes on to say that this metallic dew contains all colors. That is to say, it is the pure, white brilliance of the Primal Will. White light contains all colors, and colors, as we shall see, mark the stages of the alchemical process.

COAGULATED BY HERMETIC ART: Coagulation is defined as:

> the change from a liquid to a thickened, curd-like state, not by evaporation, but by a chemical reaction; as, the spontaneous coagulation of freshly drawn blood; the coagulation of milk by rennet, or acid, and the coagulation of egg albumin by heat; also, the reaction itself, consisting in the change of a soluble substance (usually albuminous) into an insoluble form. (*Webster*)

In Hermetic practice, coagulation is the fixation of the volatile astral light in physical forms, *as cells in the human body*. Thus the power of the dew of heaven is "turned into earth," where it becomes an integrating force. The "sweet salt" thus produced is the purified body of the adept, which has actually a sweet savor and odor.

This sweet salt is called *manna* because one spelling of the Hebrew word for "manna" is מנא. The number of this word is ninety-one, or 7 x 13, which suggests the sevenfold manifestation of the One Thing, inasmuch as thirteen is the number of the word אחד, *Achad*, UNITY.

Words corresponding to 91 in Hebrew are אמן, Amen, Faithful; יהוה אדני, *Jehovah Adonai*, Jehovah Lord; and מאכל, *Mahakal*, food, fruit. These correspondences draw attention to the relation between *food*, on the one hand, and the completeness and perfection suggested by the word "Amen" on the other. This relation is summed up in יהוה אדני, *Jehovah Adonai*, "That which was, and is, and will be, manifested as the LORD, or ruling power."

Jehovah Adonai is in one sense represented by the Hermit in Tarot, the Key corresponding to the letter Yod. When the alchemist is faithful (אמן) in perfecting the work of equilibrium whereby food (מאכל) is chemically changed in the body area corresponding to the sign Virgo, his body becomes actually the dwelling place and vehicle of Jehovah Adonai. It is then that the mighty powers of adeptship are manifested through his organism, which has become an unobstructed channel for the "Intelligence of Will" represented by the letter Yod.

ITS FATHER IS THE SUN, ITS MOTHER IS THE MOON, ETC. This is a quotation from the *Emerald Tablet*. The "Sun" is the same as the solar current of Prana described by the Yogis, and the "Moon" is the cool current of the same force which they name "Rayi." "Sun" and "Moon" also refer to the two centers of the human body named after these two light sources. The sun center is the cardiac ganglion; the moon center is the pituitary body. In the body of man these two centers specialize the First Matter for its manifestation through personality. The sun center is that which admits the cosmic fire into the house of personality. The action of the moon center does really bring enlightenment into personal consciousness.

The second paragraph of the Rosicrucian text is very clear. Remember, it refers to the "dew of heaven," which is light. This we find coagulated into solid forms, and present also in fluidic modes of manifestation. Note particularly what is said in the second sentence of this paragraph, —"it falls into the depths of the earth, and its substance is the most subtle and ethereal part of the earth." Few persons, when those words were written, had any idea that certain kinds of light penetrate deep into the earth. Few understood that light itself is the subtle substance out of which all forms are built. Even so recently as 1884, Col. Olcott was severely taken to task by British scientists for asserting that light is the fundamental substance of the physical plane. Today we have the researches of Millikan, whose work has revealed the presence of cosmic rays whose penetrating power requires the employment of thick shields of lead in order to intercept them. Alchemists will not be slow to grasp what is meant by the fact that this particular metal seems to be the one which is required to stop the passage of the cosmic rays.

COLORS OF WHITE, YELLOW, GREEN, RED, AND BLACK: Compare this with Jacob Boehme, who says:

> These are the colours wherein all things lie: blue, red, green and yellow. The fifth, white, belongs to God; and yet has also its lustre in Nature. It is the fifth essence, a pure unblemished child; as is to be seen in gold and silver, and in a white clear stone that resists fire. For fire is the proof or trial of all the colours, in which none subsists but white, the same being a reflection of God's Majesty. The black colour belongs not to the mystery of the wonders of creation, but it is the veil or the darkness wherein all things lie. (*Mysterium Pansophicum*)

Color is important in Hermetic science, and is one of the great arcana in all occultism. Until very recently, practically all published color scales have been full of "blinds", because knowledge of color is truly magical. The Rosicrucian text we are studying is no exception. The blind it employs is the substitution of black for deep indigo-blue. Boehme's "blind" consists in the use of "blue", without indicating the darkness of the shade.

The colors are the same as those given in the Hindu systems, where they are attributed to the Tattvas. Following the color names of our text, the correspondences are: WHITE, the Apas Tattva, or Water (the commonest name for the First Matter); YELLOW, the Prithivi Tattva, or Earth; GREEN, the Vayu Tattva (really a greenish blue); RED, the Tejas Tattva, Fire; BLACK, a blind for deep-indigo, the Akasha Tattva, or Quintessence.

Another attribution of colors comes from the color scale we have learned to associate with the Hebrew letters and Tarot Keys. According to that scale, WHITE is the color of undifferentiated light. YELLOW is Mercury, represented by the Magician. GREEN is the color of Venus, corresponding to the Empress. RED is that of Mars, typified by the Tower. BLACK (really deep indigo) is the color of Saturn, represented by The World.

These color correlations are very complex, and are really a field of occult study to which years of study might be devoted. For the purpose of this commentary however, and for the practical work to be undertaken in this course of lessons, the two attributions here given will suffice. To avoid confusion, remember that the first, or Tattvic attribution, applies particularly to the five subtle principles of sensation from which we construct our world picture.

CORPOREAL TO THE EXTERNAL EYE: This is to be taken at face value. The First Matter does appear to human eyes as bodies. No matter what we look at, we are seeing a form of manifestation of the Prima Materia; but the differences in the appearances of these bodies hide from us the fact that they are presentations of a single essential reality.

MINERS IN THE MOUNTAINS: Students of Hermetic science, who are engaged in the alchemical work of interior contemplation. Thus what they see is contrasted to what appears to the external eye. To them the First Matter appears to be thick, watery, and dripping. In other words, interior contemplation is not pure abstraction, or formless, at the stage represented by "mining." The miners are perfecting the activity of the *inner* sensorium, and they perceive the First Matter phenomenally. Thus we read that it "appears" to them. These interior, subjective appearances are just as real, just as valid, for scientific purposes, as the exterior, objective appearances of the physical plane. To this inner sight and touch the First Matter is a thickish, slow-moving fluid, having a tendency to form itself into globules or drops.

THE BEST DEW: The use of the superlative indicates the highest manifestation of the "dew" or light. It refers to the coagulation of the Matter as an amber colored prism in the pineal gland. This prism is made by the fusing of the granules of "brain sand" and the fusion is effected by a current of energy, or light, passing through that organ. When this prism is produced it is an actual physical stone. It may be ground to powder. It is the Transparent Jewel of the Yogis- the physical instrument which interrupts and enables us to utilize the high tension vibrations of the astral light.

THE FOURTH PARAGRAPH of the text reiterates what we have found in other alchemical writers. It emphasizes the omnipresence of the First matter, and goes on to make clear a point which is often overlooked by students of alchemy. The First Matter is *known* by the whole world. Otherwise it could not be held in contempt and rejected. What remains undiscovered by most people is its wonderful potency. It is like the sparks which fly from a cat's fur in the dark. Who, a hundred years ago, would have believed that the force thus manifested could change the face of the world, make possible instantaneous communication, give us automobiles and airplanes, enable Lindbergh to fly to Paris and Byrd to cross both poles, and multiply the actions and words of men through the agency of the radio and the talking picture? In like manner, the First Matter is present in everything, and some of its manifestations have led alchemists to the discovery of its hidden potencies. But the world at large would and does find the alchemical doctrine laughable.

TWO BRANCHES, WHITE AND RED: These are said to spring from the one root, "Y" because the development of the energy of the First Matter within the human organism is actually rooted, as we have seen, in the assimilative functions of the intestinal tract, governed by the sign Virgo, attributed to Yod.

Plate 1 in Arthur Avalon's book, *The Serpent Power*, (drawn by a Hindu artist), shows a Yogi sitting in meditation. From the Saturn center at the base of the spine rises the central line termed the Sushumna by the Yogis. On either side are shown the rising currents called Ida and Pingala. They cross each other, and remind us of the serpents on the Caduceus of Hermes.

Our crude copy of this plate does scant justice to the original, but serves to bring out the detail just mentioned. In our copy the black ascending spiral represents the red of the original. The two similar but contrasting lines, like the serpents of the caduceus, and like the pillars in the Tarot Key of the High Priestess, relate to the positive and negative currents of the life force in the body, the cool, white, lunar current (Rayi, or the alchemical moon), and the hot, red, solar current (Prana, or the alchemical sun).

The references to the rose of Jericho and the lily of the Valley of Jehoshaphat involve a very complicated piece of Qabalism, too intricate, we believe, to be included here. But it may be said that the root of the name of Jericho is a Hebrew word that means "moon," while that of Jehoshaphat has definite correspondences with the sun. Note that the red rose is associated with Jericho, or the moon, and the white lily with Jehoshaphat, or the sun. Here is an intimation that there is an interplay of apparently opposing forces.

Compare the symbolism of this paragraph with that of the lilies and roses in the garden of the Magician in the Tarot. The fundamental meaning is the same. Note also that the substance is said to *grow*, thus clearly indicating that it is a *living* substance.

THE FIFTH PARAGRAPH indicates certain dangers. Even those who know enough to seek the First Matter by looking within sometimes handle it clumsily. They "break" it by wrong forms of practice which cause "short circuits" in its flow. Ignorant workmen torture it by all sorts of silly attempts to force its natural growth too rapidly. The true artist, note well, is the passive, quiet *observer* of its influence, or inflowing. He is patient enough to wait until it is ripe, when he can gather it in its full perfection.

THE COAGULATED BLOOD OF THE RED LION: This is the lion of the 8th Tarot Key. Alchemical books mention three lions- the Green Lion, the Red Lion, and the Old Lion. The Green lion is the animal nature in its unripe, or natural state, before it has been perfected by the processes of Hermetic Art. The Red Lion is the animal nature after it has been modified and brought under control. The Green Lion becomes the Red Lion by confection with animated Mercury, say the alchemists, meaning thereby that the alchemical male or sun (the solar energy which is the actual force at work in all human activities on the physical plane) has been mixed with thought-force, called animated Mercury. In other words, the Red Lion represents the forces of the physical organism after they have been combined with what is represented by the Magician in the Tarot.

The blood of the Red Lion is actually human blood, as we are repeatedly informed by the alchemists. It is chemically different from ordinary blood. It is more highly energized, and contains subtle elements not present in ordinary blood. These elements are introduced at two points: 1) at the point of assimilation, where the substances in the chyle, or Virgin's Milk, are introduced into the bloodstream through the action of the lacteals in the small intestine; 2) in the lungs, where the blood is aerated, and where the subtle elements of the atmosphere are combined with those taken from the Virgin's Milk. Unless the subtle elements derived from food are in the bloodstream as it passes through the lungs, the other subtle elements derived from air cannot be added. For the latter will not combine with the blood unless it contains the substances derived from food.

What are these subtle elements? Various names have been given to them by alchemists, but none of the names are adequate. In time to come, they may be recognized by exoteric chemistry, and they will then be given names which will serve to identify them. Names, however, are not important. The point is that by the processes of Hermetic art we may avail ourselves of the presence of these subtle elements in food and air. Thus we may coagulate the blood of the Red Lion, and this coagulation is the fixation of these subtle elements in the substance of our brains and nervous systems, so that we become new creatures.

GLUTEN OF THE EAGLE: The Eagle, says A.E. Waite, is a name which "*has been applied by the philosophers to their Mercury after sublimation, firstly, on account of its volatility, and, secondly, because even as the eagle devours other birds, so does the Mercury of the Sages destroy, consume, and reduce even gold itself to its first matter.*"

This Eagle is the symbol of the zodiacal sign Scorpio, after reproductive energy represented by that sign, and by the letter Nun in the Hebrew alphabet, has been sublimated, or raised to its highest potency. The Yogis call the "gluten of the eagle" by the name Ojas, which means literally "the illuminating or bright." Of it Swami Vivekananda writes:

> The Yogis claim that of all the energies that the human body comprises the highest is what they call 'Ojas.' Now this Ojas is stored up in the brain, and the more the Ojas is in a man's head, the more powerful he is, the more intellectual, the more spiritually strong will that man be. This is the action of Ojas. One man may speak beautiful language and beautiful thoughts, but they do not impress people; another man speaks neither beautiful languages nor beautiful thoughts, yet his words charm. This is the power of Ojas coming out. Every movement coming from him will be powerful.
>
> Now in all mankind there is more or less of this Ojas

stored up. And all the forces that are working in the body, in their highest form, become *Ojas*. You must remember that it is only a question of transformation. The same force which is working outside, as electricity or magnetism, will become changed into inner force; the same forces that are working as muscular energy will be changed into *Ojas*. The Yogis say that that part of the human energy which is expressed as sex energy, as sexual functions, and so on, when checked and controlled, easily becomes changed into *Ojas*, and as this lowest centre is the one which guides all these functions, therefore the Yogi pays particular attention to that centre. He tries to take up all his sexual energy and covert it into *Ojas*.

We close this part of our lesson with the words of the Rosicrucian text itself: IF YOU DISCOVER IT, BE SILENT AND KEEP IT SACRED. The natural impulse, when the discovery is made, is to "tell the world," but experience shows that this is a mistaken impulse. What one knows, after making the discovery, seems so perfectly plain, so crystal clear, that there is always a great temptation to become a missionary. Actually, this knowledge is incommunicable. However clear it may be to those who possess it (and we can testify that no knowledge is clearer, that none has a greater degree of certitude) the fact remains that ordinary human language cannot possibly convey this knowledge from the mind of one having it to the mind of one unprepared to receive it.

We can be assisted by the counsel of others in our attempts to make the discovery. Each of us, notwithstanding, must make the actual discovery *alone*. Buddha had no companions under the Bo-tree. Jesus and Moses learned their final lessons in solitude, under the stars. This knowledge has its price, and the price is the personal effort of the seeker. Those who know can communicate the fact of their knowledge to each other. They signal to each other from age to age, using always code of words and symbols.

But they never *tell* the Great Secret because it never can be told. And always they warn their pupils: Cast not your pearls before swine, lest they turn and rend you.

Already, since this course has been going to our affiliates, we have had evidence that it is accomplishing its object. One writes us that we are doing everything possible to lead others to the vision of what he calls the "Eternal Sparkle." And by his very choice of words he demonstrates that he has glimpsed the Thing Itself.

Another writes:

I rejoice to tell you that *I have it now*. I have seen it in wonderful flashes many times, but now I have 'grasped it with my mind' and have faith that I can hold it. I didn't get it *all* from the alchemical quotations. In fact I had been reaching out for it all through the Basic Course, but— the *Hermit* was the lesson that I got the *least* out of in the whole course! Last night, after reading my second lesson, I saw 'men like trees walking'; and I said, 'Several of these quotations are in The Hermit. Perhaps he will throw more light on the mystery.'

So I re-read the Hermit– *devoured* it, I should say– hungrily. And there it was, all so plain and clear; so intelligible; so exactly what I had been groping for in vain. And now- I know that whereas I was blind when I studied that ninth lesson nearly a year ago— now I see...

A few words, in closing, about the mental attitude that prepares one for this discovery. You will notice that the letter just quoted speaks of "reaching out for it," and of "groping for it." It also intimates that the writer was *hungry* for the illumination. Compare this with Boehme's statement:

I am not a master of literature nor of arts, such as belong to this world, but a foolish and simple-minded man. I have never desired to learn any sciences, but from early youth I strove after the salvation of my soul, and thought how I might inherit or possess the kingdom of heaven. Now while I was wrestling and battling, being aided by God, a wonderful light arose within my soul. It was a light entirely foreign to my unruly nature, but in it I recognized the true nature of God and man, and the relation existing between them, a thing which heretofore I had never understood, and far which I would never have sought.

This discovery comes about through the awakening of the function of the "Third Eye," as it is often called. This is the brain center which we also call the "Adytum," or "Secret place of the Most High." Its bodily correspondence is the pineal gland. Its function is expressed in direct knowledge of the fiery essence hidden behind the manifold veils of physical form.

The awakening comes to those who are hungry for it, to those who wrestle and battle for it, to those who will not be content with anything less. But, paradoxically, it does not come in moments of stress and struggle. The hunger, the wrestling, the battling- these are but the preparation. Thus we are told, in *Light on the Path*:

> Look for the flower to bloom in the silence that follows the storm; not till then. It shall grow, it will shoot up, it will make branches and leaves and form buds, while the storm continues, while the battle lasts. But not till the whole personality of the man is dissolved and melted- not until it is held by the divine fragment which has created it, as a mere subject for grave experiment and experience- not until the whole nature has yielded and become subject unto its higher self, can the bloom open. Then will come a calm such as comes in a tropical country after the heavy rain, when nature works so swiftly that one may see her action. Such a calm will come to the harassed spirit. And in the deep silence the mysterious event will occur which will prove that the way has been found. Call it by what name you will, it is

a voice that speaks where there is none to speak - it is a messenger that comes, a messenger without form or substance; or it is the flower of the soul that has opened. It cannot be described by any metaphor.

Readers who possess the Tarot may assist themselves in their quest for the perception of the First Matter by using these Keys as means of evoking their hidden interior knowledge of it:

0. THE FOOL: This represents the most abstract aspect of the First Matter, its unconditioned essence.

1. THE MAGICIAN: This corresponds to what the alchemists term "their" Mercury.

2. THE HIGH PRIESTESS: This symbolizes the Virgin Sperm of the World, the Catholic Magnesia, and the Diana of the Wise.

3. THE EMPRESS: This represents the First Matter as the mother or matrix of all things in this world, "the soft, prolific Venus," as Thomas Vaughan says.

Look at one of these Keys at a time. Do not try to guess what it means. Endeavor to absorb yourself in it, with the idea that it shall draw forth ideas from the depths of your mind. As the ideas come, make notes of them.

Be sure, also, to make yourself more and more familiar with the words of the sages given in Lesson Two. It is a good plan to read several of these quotations before concentrating on the Tarot Key you have selected for the day's experiment.

The next lesson will deal with the three alchemical principles: Sulfur, Mercury, and Salt.

IV
THE THREE PRINCIPLES

*A*s you learned in the first lesson, there is a close parallel between the yoga doctrine concerning the three gunas, or qualities, and the alchemical teaching concerning the three principles. In that lesson you were told that the Sattvaguna corresponds to the alchemical Mercury, the Rajasguna to alchemical Sulfur, and the Tamasguna to alchemical Salt. We shall now proceed to a further exposition of the nature of these three principles or qualities.

Sattva means literally, "illumination material," or the essence of enlightenment. In his translation of the Bhagavad Gita, Charles Johnston calls it Substance, and renders the sixth verse of the fourteenth chapter as follows: "Substance, luminous through its stainlessness, and free from sorrow, binds by the bond of pleasure and the bond of knowledge." He translates the eleventh verse of the same chapter thus: "When light shines in at all the doors in this dwelling, when wisdom shines, then let him know that Substance has prevailed." Again: "The fruit of works well done is stainless, belonging to Substance...From Substance is born wisdom...Those who dwell in Substance go upward."

Johnston's translation of Sattva as "Substance" is valuable to us because he is a thorough Sanskritist, and we may be sure that he did not decide on this English rendering without weighing the matter carefully. Thus it becomes evident that Sattva is very like what we have been considering in the two preceding lessons under the designation of First Matter, which, you will remember, is called Mercury by Kelly, Philalethes, Albertus Magnus, Raymond

Lully, and many other alchemists. In other words, there is no difference between the First Matter and the first of the three principles.

Whether we call the first principle Sattva or Mercury, we are to think of it as a luminous substance. Thus we can understand why the alchemical treatise *Aesch Mezareph*, the Book of Purifying Fire, attributes the principle Mercury to Kether, the Crown, the highest of the ten aspects of the Life-power composing the Tree of Life.

On the diagram of the Tree of Life, the Crown is represented as a sphere of brilliant white at the top of the diagram. It is called the Crown because it is the supreme or ruling principle; but it has other names which clearly indicate its identity with Sattva, or "illumination material," among them are: אור מופלא , *Aur Mopeleh*, Hidden Light; אור פשוט, *Aur Pawshut*, Simplest Light; and אור פנימי, *Aur Penimi*, Inner Light.

Qabalists declare that Limitless Light, *Ain Soph Aur*, condenses itself in Kether, and sets up a whirling motion which is the beginning of manifestation. Thus the initial activity of the Life-power is represented as the selection of a point at which to begin, so that Kether is termed נקודה ראשונה, *Nequdeh Rashuneh*, the Primordial Point, and this point is said to be the root of all manifestation. Like the First Matter, it is also called the "Existence of Existences," and the "Concealed of the Concealed."

What we wish to emphasize just here is that these Qabalistic doctrines are by no means mere philosophical abstractions. Hebrew Wisdom, like yoga and alchemy, is founded upon human experience, and that experience is the direct perception of a self-luminous substance as the root of all things, the self sustaining existence (or better, *subsistence*) which enters into all forms whatsoever. Furthermore, it is perceived as essentially identical with the energy which produces the physical manifestations of light.

It is to the purest state of this subsistent light that Hindus give the name Sattva, and alchemists the name Mercury.

> The first is Sattvaguna, the function of which, relative to the other gunas, is to *reveal* consciousness. The greater the presence or the power of Sattvaguna, the greater the approach to the condition of Pure Consciousness...The truly Sattvik man is a divine man, his temperament being called in the Tantras Divyabhava. Through Sattvaguna passage is made to Sat, which is Chit or Pure Consciousness, by the Siddhayogi, who is identified with Pure Spirit. (Arthur Avalon, *The Serpent Power*)

It is also said by Hindu authorities that Prakriti or Shakti (First Matter) in its aspect of Perfect Unity is the divine perception which is pure Sattva and attribute of Ishvara, the Supreme Self.

Ishvara is defined by Vivekandanda as: "The Supreme Ruler; the highest possible conception, through reason, of the Absolute, which is beyond all thought." This conception is precisely what is behind the Qabalistic term יחידה, *Jechidah*, the Indivisible, which also designates the Supreme Ruler, or ONE IDENTITY, attributed to Kether.

The Sattvaguna also predominates in what Hindus call Buddhi, the principle of determination, concerning which it is written that Buddhi, the basis of all cognition, sensation, and resolves, is the charioteer; Manas, the deliberative faculty of the mind, the reins; and the senses, the horses. That is to say, Buddhi is the driver of the chariot in the seventh Key of Tarot, and in this sense Buddhi is indistinguishable from Ishvara or Yechideh, the true self. What we must keep continually before us, in this connection, is the fact that this One Self is itself identical with the Limitless Light concentrated in the Small Point of original manifestation. In other words, the Self is a point of manifestation for a dynamic energy, a point *through* which the energy is continually passing. It is the tendency of our minds to think of the Self or I AM, as being something static or fixed, but Ageless Wisdom declares the opposite. It may help us to recall the geometrical definition of a point- "simple location, without length, breadth, or thickness." In other words, nothing whatever that has shape, size or form.

This conception is beyond our mental grasp. Thus we are told that the *residuum* after all grasping is at an end is the true Self. True knowledge causes even this Self to vanish. It is swallowed up in the infinity of the Limitless Light, the radiant energy which is termed by Qabalists Ain Soph Aur, and by Hindus, Mulaprakriti, the root-matter.

We have just said that Sattva, or alchemical Mercury, is the attribute of Ishvara or Yechideh. Here it is interesting to note that the numeral value of יחידה, Yechideh, is thirty-seven, which we have seen to be the number of degrees in the angle which determines the relation of the hypotenuse of a Pythagorean triangle to its base. (Lesson Three, p56) In other words, the number thirty-seven signifies the power which maintains the relation of the evolving forms of the Life-power to Isis, or Mother Nature. That same power is Yechideh, the Self.

With this in mind, let us analyze the geometrical properties of the Mercury symbol shown in the margin. We find: 1) a semicircle, corresponding to the number eleven; 2) a circle, corresponding to the number twent-two; 3) a cross composed of two lines, each representing the number two, so that the cross stands for four. (In occult geometry any circle is twenty-two, because of the approximate Pi-proportion which makes a circle three and one-seventh times its diameter. Thus the smallest whole number which can represent a diameter is seven, corresponding to a circumference of twenty-two. The valuation of the semicircle as eleven is derived in the same way. Readers of these pages are probably also familiar with the Pythagorean dictum that any line is the geometrical equivalent of the number two. If, then, we add together the numbers corresponding to the parts of the Mercury symbol, the total is thirty-seven.

After all this, it should be evident that the name "Mercury" was deliberately chosen for the first principle because of its mythological associations. Mercury, or Hermes, was the messenger of the gods. It was his office to *reveal* the divine will, just as it is the office of the Sattvaguna to reveal consciousness. Mercury invented all the arts and sciences, and so corresponds to the determinative faculty, Buddhi. In particular he revealed the arts of astrology, magic, and alchemy, and every one of these, rightly understood, has for its object the maintenance of the true relation of evolving form to the fundamental characteristics of Mother Isis, or Nature. In the forms of life below man, this determinative power is exercised upon the vehicles of life without their conscious cooperation. In man there is conscious awareness of what is going on, which leads to his voluntary cooperation in the process, which results finally in the perfect unification of his consciousness with that of the Originating Principle, as shown in Lesson Three, p55.

In that diagram, the first of the three divisions of the line corresponding to Osiris is attributed to Mercury, because the first differentiation of the One Life-power is this same principle of pure knowing, Sattva or Mercury.

This principle is that aspect of the Life-power which has been termed super consciousness throughout the lessons issued by the School of Ageless Wisdom. Super consciousness is the plane of life-activity above the level of human self-conscious knowing; but when we call it a plane we must again be careful not to fall into the error of supposing it to be static. It is a field of intense activity, a sphere of vibratory movement, a region of energy beyond the limits of our ordinary awareness.

That energy is the true Mercury of the sages. It is the power which flows down from above into the uplifted wand of the Magician in Key One of Tarot. A power invisible and intangible, but a real power, nevertheless. A power which becomes manifest on the physical plane as light, the Great Magical Agent described by Eliphas Levi. A power hidden behind the manifold veils of name and form. A power perfectly simple and indivisible in itself, but seemingly subdivided into an intricate criss-cross of complex manifestations. A power which is correctly described as Inner Light, which may become actually visible to the awakened inner sensorium of the alchemist as he progresses toward the completion of the Great Work.

Rajas, the second of the three qualities, is rendered "Force" by Johnston. In his translation of the fourteenth chapter of the Bhagavad Gita we read: "Force, of the essence of desire, engendering thirst and attachment, binds the lord of the body by the bond of works... Desire of possessions, activity, the undertaking of works, restlessness, longing, these are born when Force prevails... The fruit of Force is pain... In the midst stand those who dwell in Force." Arthur Avalon writes: "The function of Rajasguna is to *make active* – that is, it works on Tamas to suppress Sattva, or on Sattva to suppress Tamas."

Compare this with the words of Jacob Boehme: "The wise heathen have in some measure understood this ground, for they say, that in *Sulfur*, *Mercury*, and *Sal*, all things in this world consist; wherein they have not looked upon the matter only, but upon the spirit; for the ground of it consisteth not in gross salt, quicksilver, and brimstone, they mean not so, but they mean the spirit of such properties; in that, everything indeed consisteth, whatsoever liveth and groweth and hath being in this world, whether it be spiritual or material.

> For they understand by Salt the sharp magnetical desire of nature; and by Mercury, they mean the motion and separation of nature, by which everything is marked with its own image and shape; and by Sulfur they mean the sensible, desiring, and grown life. (*Clavis*, p82)

The Rajasguna is active in that manifestation of the Life-power which the Hindus call Ahangkara, the "I-maker." Ahangkara is the realization of oneself as a person. It is the self-consciousness of worldly experience, in which one thinks of oneself as a particular person who stands in relation with the objects of his experience. It is the power that Johnston, in his translation of the Gita, calls "self-reference."

According to alchemical doctrine, the office of the principle named Sulfur is to swallow and transmute Mercury. This idea is presented under many curious veils of symbolism, but one need not enter into an elaborate examination of these. The meaning should be clear in the light of what has just been written. The alchemical Sulfur is the active principle of self-consciousness, and the office of this is to bring down the superconscious energy (Mercury) so that it may be assimilated.

In Tarot, therefore, the invisible force which is drawn down from above by the Magician is Mercury, and Sulfur is represented by his red robe, typifying action. Superconscious energy is the true food of self-consciousness, which differentiates the Mercury so received into various forms of self-conscious activity. Thus the Hindus tell us that in the operation of Ahangkara (self-consciousness), Buddhi, in which the Sattva quality (Mercury) prevails, is the principle.

In the *Book of Purifying Fire*, the alchemical Sulfur is attributed to the second aspect of the Life-power, named

Chokmah, or Wisdom, Chokmah is understood as signifying practical as well as theoretical wisdom. It is not merely the distilled essence of experience. It is power to do, power to make active, and thus exactly corresponds to the nature of Sulfur and the Rajasguna.

In human personality, Chokmah is declared to be the seat of the vital force. This vital force is the "spiritual seed of Sulfur," mentioned by Ripley and other alchemists.

They also declare that this seed is their secret fire. This corresponds to the Qabalistic doctrine that Chokmah is the "Root of Fire." It agrees also with the statement of the alchemist El-Habib, who says that in the tincture, Sulfur is the part of fire.

The noun "tincture," in its alchemical sense, means "mixture of colors." It is a fairly obvious figure of speech for human personality. The tincture is contained in the philosophical egg. This is the human aura, seen by those who have awakened the inner sensorium, as an ovoid, transparent body in which there is a continual play of colors. This philosophical egg, containing Mercury, Sulfur and Salt, is the "vessel of glass" in which the matter of the work is brought to perfection.

Raymond Lully says that the true philosophical Sulfur is not to be sensibly distinguished from the true Mercury. The same writer also insists that the living Sulfur has no connection whatsoever with the ordinary substance bearing the same name. Again, in various alchemical writings, one reads that the Sulfur of Sol is the Soul of Gold, that the Sulfur of the Moon is the Soul of Silver, and so with the other metals. Spenser gives us a key to this in the lines:

> Fore of the soule the bodie forme doth take;
> For soule is forme and doth the bodie make.

That is to say, Sulfur is the power of formation, inherent in the Life Force. Here, again, we have confirmation from the Qabalah, for Chokmah, to which Sulfur is attributed, is said also to be בחכמה, *Kachmeh*, the power of formation. The Universal Sulfur is therefore said to be the light from which all particular sulfurs proceed. Thus Boehme says:

> All life and motion, with understanding, reason and senses, both in animals and vegetables, consist originally in Sulfur, viz. in nature's desire...Man, and every life also, as to the kingdom of this world, was created and generated out of the outward Sulfur; man out of the inward Sulfur, and the outward creature only out of the outward...Whatever grows, lives, and moves in this world, consists in Sulfur, and Mercury is the life in Sulfur, and the Salt is the corporeal being of Mercury's hunger. (Condensed from *Signatura Rerum*)

The alchemical Sulfur, then, is to be regarded as the middle principle. Thus its symbol is assigned to the second of the three divisions of the Osiris line in the Pythagorean triangle. Mercury is the Spirit, and Sulfur is the Soul, in all forms of the Life-power's manifestation. Hence Mercury corresponds to what the Greeks term *Pneuma*, and Sulfur is what they designate as *Psyche*. As the yogis declare, this principle stands in the midst, as the quality which may act upon Sattva to suppress Tamas, or upon Tamas to suppress Sattva. It may operate in either direction.

In the natural man it feeds upon Tamas, upon the bodily sensations, which are below it in the scale of consciousness. It is then drawn into the conflicts of sensation which are called the brimstone fires of hell.

In the spiritual, or "pneumatic," man who has entered upon the performance of the Great Work, this principle opens itself to the descending power of the Sattva quality, or Mercury, which is its proper food. This leads to the regeneration which is the object of the Great Work. Hence Boehme says that Sulfur is the womb whereinto we must enter, if we would be new born.

Sulfur, active in the desiring and growing life of self-consciousness, works either for the gratification of the senses, or for man's release from this bondage. Sulfur is that in us which drives us to undertake works that shall lead us to higher levels. It is the transforming power, represented by the Tarot Magician in his red robe.

The Tarot Keys make this clear. If you are familiar with them, you will remember that Key Four, the Emperor, is explained as representing the same essential power as the Magician. The Emperor is the Magician, after the Magician's mating with the High Priestess has transformed her into the Empress. In all the older Tarot packs, as in the B.O.T.A. version, the composition of the picture of the Emperor is based upon the symbol of Sulfur shown in the margin — a triangle surmounting a cross. The same figure is also the basis of the design of Key Seven, the Chariot, except that a square, forming the body of the chariot, encloses the cross.

There are two ways to analyze the Sulfur symbol. One is to consider each of its five lines as representing the number two. Then the whole symbol corresponds to the number ten. The other is to think of the symbol as a triangle (three) surmounting a cross (four). Then the number represented by the symbol will be seven. Every student of these pages who is familiar with the esoteric meaning of the numbers will see that there is a close correspondence between ten and seven. In Tarot, seven and ten are the third and fourth terms of the series of Keys which begins with one, the Magician, and includes 1, 4, 7, 10, 13, 16, and 19. Every card in this series has some reference to alchemical Sulfur.

Key One is Sulfur as the transforming power. Key Four shows it as the martial, regulative power of the Constituting Intelligence. Key Ten represents it as the whirling motion which makes all things active, the fly-wheel, one might say, of nature's mechanism. Key Thirteen represents it as the power of growth associated with the meanings of the letter Nun, and presents it symbolically as the power which produces the outward phenomena of death and change. Key Sixteen shows it as the lightning-flash, destroying the structures of error. Key Nineteen is a symbol of the regeneration effected by the Great Work, a symbol of the making of philosophical Gold, or Sol; and in connection with this Key of Tarot we may remember that Bernard of Trevisan says: "Gold (Sol) is nothing but quicksilver congealed by its Sulfur."

The Hebrew noun for Sulfur is גפרית, *Gofreeth*. Observe that the letters composing it are G, referred to the Moon, P, referred to Mars, R, referred to the Sun, I, referred to the operation of Mercury in Virgo, and Th, referred to Saturn. The Moon center is the pituitary body. The Mars center is that which governs the reproductive functions. The Sun center is that which is directly connected with the action of the heart, with the function of the spleen, and with the admission of solar energy into the sphere of personality. The operation of Mercury in Virgo has been explained in connection with the First Matter. The Saturn center is that in which the Kundalini force, or secret fire, is coiled, and is that also which controls excretion and the orgasm which occurs at the climax of the sex function.

Modern knowledge of the functions of the glands makes it evident that the parts of the body represented by the letters of גפרית are actually those which are fundamental in all the activities of personality. It is by the forces operating through these centers that all human work is done. We do not go so far as to say that the word was intentionally spelled this way in order to preserve ancient knowledge of these centers and their functions, although we do know that modern "discoveries" in this field are but the uncovering of what has been known before. All that we assert is, that whether by change or intention, the letters of גפרית do actually correspond to parts of the human organism which are actively concerned in alchemical work. In this connection the student should remember that the uplifted wand in the Magician's hand is a phallic symbol, which has been explained in our works on Tarot as typifying the sublimation and modification of the forces ordinarily employed in physical reproduction.

Self-consciousness (Sulfur), on account of its identification with the desire-nature, is inseparable from those basic activities of the human organism which have to do with the perpetuation of the species. It is an open secret nowadays that the alchemical process is one which utilizes the nerve-force which energizes the organs of reproduction, and diverts its activity to effect chemical and structural changes in the alchemist's own body. The Kundalini force, or serpent power, coiled in the Saturn center at the base of the spine, is the electric fire which fuses the brain-sand in the pineal gland into the crystal which is the true Philosophers' Stone. Subtle modifications of the bloodstream by the internal secretions of the gonads, under the rulership of the Mars center, and of the pituitary body, or Moon center, are a necessary part of the Great Work. So is the charging of the bloodstream with certain elements derived from food in the region of the body corresponding to the operations of Mercury in Virgo. Indispensable to the success of the operation, also, is the function of the Sun center near the heart. All these activities are under the control of Sulfur, or the Rajasguna, when it works on Sattva (Mercury) to suppress the operation of Tamas (Salt).

Johnston translates Tamas as "Darkness." In his version of the fourteenth chapter of the Gita we read: "Darkness, born of unwisdom is known to be the deluder of all who are embodied; it binds through heedlessness, indo-

lence and sleep...Darkness, enwrapping wisdom, causes
attachment through sloth...Obscurity, inactivity, sloth, delusion, these are born when Darkness prevails...The fruit
of Darkness is unwisdom...Those who dwell in Darkness
go downward, under the sway of the lowest powers."

Hence Boehme, who calls this principle *Sal*, or Salt,
declares it to be the intense magnetical desire of nature,
which draws the Life Force down into itself. Nature here
should be understood as being represented by the base-
line of the Pythagorean triangle, into which the stream of
cosmic energy represented by the vertical line corresponding to Osiris descends, to be involved in the forms of the
four elements, represented by the four divisions of the Isis
line. Boehme says also:

> Whatever grows, lives, and moves in this world, consists in
> Sulfur, and Mercury is the life in Sulfur, and the Salt is
> the corporeal being of Mercury's hunger, though the body is
> manifold. The outward world's desire is in Sulfur, Mercury,
> and Sal; for such an essence it is in itself, viz. a hunger after
> itself, and is also its own satisfying; for the Sul desires Phur,
> and Phur desires Mercury, and both these desire Sal; for Sal
> is their son, which they hatch in their desire, and afterwards
> becomes their habitation, and also food. Each desire desires
> only the essentiality of Salt according to its property; for
> Salt is diverse; one part is sharpness or cold, and one part
> sharpness of heat; also one part brimstone; and one part
> salniter from Mercury.

Boehme, it will be noted, divides Sulfur into a twofold
nature. He represents its union with that which is above
it (Mercury : Sattva) by the syllable Sul, which he calls
the "oil of nature, wherein the life burns, and everything
grows." Its union with that which is below it (Salt : Tamas)
he represents by the syllable Phur as being the "desire
of the free *lubet*." This word lubet is used by Law, in his
translation of Boehme, for the original German *lust*. It is
practically the same as the *libido* of analytical psychology.

Boehme also clearly indicates his knowledge that the lowest of the three principles partakes of the qualities of those above it, when he says that Salt is one part brimstone (Sulfur) and one part salniter from Mercury. Observe, too, that he recognizes a pair of opposites in Salt: sharpness, or intensity, of heat, and sharpness of cold, viz. extremes of expansion (heat) and contraction (cold).

Ordinary salt retards the chemical processes which cause decay. On account of this it is used to preserve meat. This is what is regarded as the main characteristic of al-chemical Salt. It is due to the quality of inertia attributed to Tamas in Hindu philosophy. This quality is definitely associated with the idea of *body*.

Thus Paracelsus writes: "Hermes truly said that all the seven metals were made and compounded of three sub-stances, and in like manner also tinctures (understand *bodies* — P.C.) and the Philosophers' Stone. These three substances he names Spirit, Soul, and Body.. Now, in order that these three distinct substances may be rightly under-stood, namely, spirit, soul, and body, it should be known that they signify nothing else than the three principles, Mercury, Sulfur, and Salt, from which all the seven metals are generated. For Mercury is the spirit, Sulfur is the soul, and Salt is the body. The metal between the spirit and the body, concerning which Hermes speaks, is the soul, which indeed is Sulfur. It unites these two contraries, the body and the spirit, and changes them into one essence."

Paracelsus also declares that the properties of Salt are compaction, coagulation, and unification. And he writes: "Know that Salt is a balsam, and conserves Mercury so that its properties shall not putrefy or decay."

In the book *Aesch Mezareph* the principle Salt is at-tributed to the third aspect of the Life-power, *Binah*, or Understanding. On the Tree of Life Binah is represented as a black circle, the color corresponding to the idea of

Salt or Tamas as the principle of Darkness. Binah is the Great Mother, or dark womb of manifestation. Binah is also called the Great Sea, which is characterized by its saltiness. This aspect of the Life-power is clearly indicated to be the source of all embodiment, throughout the Qabalistic philosophy.

Binah is the diversifying power, which produces the *appearance* of multiplication of bodies throughout the universe. Its real action is to veil consciousness, and thus produce world-experience. Thus it corresponds exactly to what Hindus call Shakti (Power) in its aspect of Maya. Thus Arthur Avalon writes:

> Maya Shakti is that which seemingly makes the whole (Purna) into the not-whole (Apurna), the infinite into the finite, the formless into forms, and the like. It is a power which thus cuts down, veils and negates. Negates what? Perfect consciousness. (*The Serpent Power*)

He also says:

> The general action of Shakti is to veil consciousness...In fact, like the *materia prima* of the Thomistic philosophy, it is a *finitising* principle. To all seeming, it finitises and makes form in the infinite formless Consciousness. So do all the gunas. But one does it less and another more. The function of Tamasguna is to suppress and *veil* consciousness... The lower descent is made in the scale of nature the more Tamasguna prevails, as in so-called 'brute substance,' which has been supposed to be altogether inert.

Now this is precisely the import of the essential Qabalistic teaching about Binah, the lowest, or outermost, of the "Three Supernals" among the Sephiroth. Binah is the same as the Thomistic finitizing *prima materia*. Throughout the Qabalah the Great Mother is described in language such as Hindus invariably apply to Shakti as Maya. Even the English translation of the word Binah- "Understanding" – means by derivation exactly the same as "Substance," literally, "that which stands under."

This is true even though Binah is said to be the seat of the higher soul, *Neshamah*, through which one receives the interior teaching by the operation of intuition. The point is that even the highest instruction is yet a veil for the Absolute Reality. Whether it come from without or from within, teaching is but a preliminary to true illumination. As Eliphas Levi says, revelation is really a revealing. Hence the power of the Tamasguna may be discerned even at these high levels, since there can be no instruction without form, no communication without the dualism of speaker and hearer, and thus no intuition without some tinge of Avidya, or unwisdom.

The Hindu point of view, which often regards the appearances of finite existence as unmitigated evils, is reflected in the view that the Tamasguna is also evil. This is an erroneous opinion, however, because all the older sages are agreed that some mixture of the Tamasguna is present even in the highest aspects of divinity, so long as there is any manifestation whatever.

The *relative* evil from which both yoga and alchemy seek to deliver us is the undue *predominance* of Salt or Tamas. In the Western schools of Ageless Wisdom this is emphasized. Thus, although Salt is used in the story of Lot's wife to represent the crystallizing and limiting consequences of that mistaken mental attitude which always harks back to precedent and to the conditions of past experience, we find that Jesus compares his pupils to the same principle, on account of its preservative quality.

In the Qabalah, too, the usefulness of Salt is emphasized. The Hebrew word for it is מלח, *melekh*, which is referred originally to the sea itself, from a verbal form, spelled with the same letters, meaning to flow, to dissolve, to vanish away. In Aramaic, the same combination of letters is used for a verb meaning "to subsist." The idea is that subsistence, or manifestation, is really an eternal flux, even as the Greek philosopher, Heraclitus, asserted.

But מלה has the value of seventy-eight, and this is three times twenty-six, or יהוה, "That which was, is and will be." Thus מלה is a numerical formula of the threefold manifestation of reality. Readers of these pages who are familiar with the conceptions of the constitution of matter which have been developed during the last thirty years under the influence of such thinkers as Planck, Einstein, Heisenberg, Dirac, and others, will see that here we approach the ideas which have been forced upon physicists by their mathematical analysis of the results of strictly scientific laboratory research. [1]

By Gematria, or correspondence of words to the same number, the noun מלה is equivalent to חנך, *Enoch*, the name of the patriarch who "walked with God." This proper name means "initiation." Another word equivalent to מלה is לחם, *Lechem*, food or bread. (Here note that the birthplace of Jesus, whose name signifies, "Reality Liberates," is in Bethlehem, בית-לחם, "the house of food." This corresponds to what has been said already about the importance of the Virgo area of the human body, in which the assimilation of food is carried out. And it may also give some light on the real significance of the dogma of Jesus' virgin birth).

Finally, מלה, by Gematria, is equivalent to מזלא, *Mezla*, a Qabalistic term designating the descending power flowing from Kether, the Crown. The literal meaning of *mezla* is "to drip, to flow down in drops." Mezla, for Qabalists, is the same as Shakti for yogis. As Shakti produces the seeming multiplicity of appearances, so mezla produces all the manifold aspects of being which are summarized in the ten circles of the Tree of Life, representing the ten aspects

---

1. One of the most popular presentations of these new attitudes of physical science and of some of their philosophical consequences is *The Mysterious Universe*, by Sir James Jeans (Macmillan Co, 1930).

of the One Identity, and the twenty-two connecting paths, representing the forces of consciousness attributed to the Hebrew letters.

The number seventy-eight, moreover, is the sum of the numbers from one to twelve, and may therefore be taken to relate to the twelve lines which bound a cube. Ordinary salt crystallizes into perfect cubes, and representations of the cube are shown in Tarot Keys 2, 4, and 7. In the *Basic Tarot Course* they have been explained as representing the physical plane, or world of embodiment, and as being also representations of the word יהוה, Jehovah, inasmuch as the numbers which designate the limitations of a cube (six faces, eight points, and twelve lines), add up to twenty-six, the number of יהוה.

This numeral symbolism may seem rather complicated to some who are taking this course. But it should be considered very carefully. In the performance of the Great Work, as in ordinary chemistry, numeral formulas have an important part. The science of sacred numeration (as distinguished from its divinatory counterfeits) will, we hope, be more adequately dealt with in future publications of the School of Ageless Wisdom. At present we need only say that the better you understand the numeral correlations given here and there through our work, the more evident will become the real inner significance of much of this instruction. In the present instance, the various considerations that have been developed from the number seventy-eight, as applying to Salt, all point to the idea that this lowest of the three principles is really just as truly an aspect of Reality as either of the others.

The truth is that the ONE REALITY HAS THE POWER OF FINITIZING ITSELF through the operation of the Tamasguna or Salt. That this principle does produce inertia and darkness, that it is the principle of embodiment which veils consciousness, is undoubtedly true. Thus, if we add the digits of seventy-eight, we get fifteen, and this is the number of the Tarot Key named THE DEVIL. That Key represents the exoteric ideas which are held in respect to the Tamasguna, and these exoteric ideas sometimes affect men of considerable enlightenment. Thus Mohini Chatterji, in his commentary on the Gita, explicitly identifies Tamas with "badness;" and even Swami Vivekananda permits himself to speak of "getting rid" of this quality.

The real esoteric doctrine is that Tamas is just as useful as any of the other principles. Its preponderance, to the point of extinguishing the operation of Sattva in our lives, is what we seek to overcome. By right use of Sulfur the alchemist effects an equilibration between Mercury and Salt. Note, an *equilibration*. It would be just as unfortunate to have the balance tipped too far on the side of Mercury, or Sattva, even though it has been said that the divine man is "Sattvik."

⊖ The fundamental idea in the Great Work is the maintenance of equilibrium, and that idea is suggested by the symmetrical symbol representing Salt. This shows clearly the balance between that which is above and that which is below. If the line be valued as two, then the symbol stands for the number twenty-four, and for the words: גויה, substance, a body; רו, abundance; and כד, a pot, a large earthenware vessel. The significance of these words in relation to Salt is plain. But if the line be taken as a diameter (seven), then the figure stands for the number twenty-nine, corresponding to the words: הדך, to break down, to overturn; and כבב, to spin, to bind together. These, because alchemical Salt has both these properties of destruction and correlation.

The preliminary processes of the Great Work consist in the union of Sulfur with Mercury (Rajas with Sattva) to overcome the inertia, darkness, and heaviness of Salt

(Tamas).

Little by little, through the influx of power from the super conscious level (Mercury), effected by control of thought and action at the self-conscious level (Sulfur), the preponderance of fixed, habitual subconscious impulses (Salt) over self-conscious determinations (Sulfur) is overcome. Eventually the subconscious level of the Life-power's activity is purged and purified. Its fixed conditions are volatilized (that is, its complexes are dissolved), and new and beneficent fixations ensue under the influx of the super conscious powers.

Mastery of subconsciousness (Salt) is not brought about by dissolving all complexes and keeping them dissolved. On the contrary, *we must have complexes*. A complex is simply a group of mental forces clustered around a nucleus. What we are to get rid of is the wrong kind of complexes.

The first steps in yoga and alchemy have to do with their dissolution. In yoga: 1) *Yama*, non-killing, truthfulness, non-stealing, continence, non-receiving of gifts; 2) *Niyama*, cleanliness, contentment, self-control, study, devotion; 3) *Asana*, posture and muscular control; 4) *Pranayama*, control of nerve-currents through regulation of breath; 5) *Pratyahara*, observation of the workings of the mind, similar to the catharsis of analytical psychology. In alchemy: 1) *Calcination*, the purgation of the "Stone," by a gentle heat which expels the volatile matters; 2) *Dissolution*, the breaking up of complexes, through works similar to Niyama; 3) *Separation*, akin to the first stages of Pratyahara, wherein the flow of ideas is observed; 4) *Conjunction*, a second stage of Pratyahara, in which the philosophical Man and Woman are united. A hint of this is given in the symbolism of the sixth Key of Tarot, THE LOVERS; but the final stage of this work of Conjunction is represented by The Hermit (whose letter, Yod, signifies

Coition or *Copulation*). 5) *Putrefaction*, closely related to Pranayama, which, by changing the nerve-currents in the body, affects also the subtle states of subconsciousness, and dissolves still further the complexes which retard free life-expression.

We do not mean to say that the stages of yoga, as commonly given, are precisely the same as the alchemical processes — the same in order, that is. All that is intended here is to show that both forms of the one art deal with purification, equilibration, and transformation, and that purification comes first. That which is purified is really the Tamasguna, or Salt, the subconscious level of the Life-power's self expression.

Summing up then, we may say:

1. That Mercury, or Sattvaguna, is the super conscious level of life, corresponding to the highest of the three Supernals on the Tree of Life, Kether, the Crown. In another kind of symbolic expression, the Mercury of the sages is represented by the Tarot FOOL.

2. That Sulfur, or Rajasguna, is the self-conscious level, corresponding to Chokmah, the seat of the Life Force. In the Tarot Keys this aspect of consciousness is represented primarily by the MAGICIAN, but all the Keys in the sequence including 1, 4, 7, 10, 13, 16, and 19 are symbols of alchemical Sulfur. As Boehme indicates by dividing the word into its two syllables, Sul and Phur, this principle works both ways. In combination with that which is below it, it works to veil consciousness by inertia, and lowers the level of personal consciousness. In combination with that which is above it, it works to unveil consciousness by illumination, and thus raises the level of personal awareness. Sulfur is therefore the actual transforming power.

3. That Salt, or Tamasguna, is the subconscious level, corresponding to Binah, the Great Sea of Substance, on the Tree of Life. In the Tarot Keys this principle is primarily represented by the HIGH PRIESTESS. In a certain recondite sense, however, Salt is represented also by the following pairs of Keys: 2 and 3; 5 and 6; 8 and 9; 11 and 12; 14 and 15; 17 and 18; 20 and 21. For all these Keys represent the working of forces which are chiefly subconscious, or below the threshold of self-conscious awareness.

From these considerations, it will be apparent that the burden of the Great Work falls on Sulfur. Thus we read this summation of the whole operation in *The Book of Lambspring*: "Cook the Sulphur well with Sulphur." So also Ripley tells us that the spiritual seed of Sulfur is the secret Fire, burning in the Athanor, the unique chemical instrument, or alchemical furnace, whose name itself means "Essence of Fire."

When the self-conscious level of personality is rightly understood and utilized, it acts, even as shown in Key One of Tarot, as a mediator and transformer. Then the Sulfur assimilates, or swallows, the Mercury of the sages. In consequence of this, the Salt is purified, after having passed through the stages mentioned. In plain language, subconscious states of mind are modified, and the power of subconsciousness to build physical structure and control the functions of the body is turned in the right direction.

This, you will see, is quite another interpretation of alchemy from those given by Mrs. Atwood and Ethan Allen Hitchcock. The former thought of alchemy as a sort of hypnotism, performed by the alchemist upon a patient other than himself, whereby clairvoyant lucidity may be produced. Hitchcock supposed that alchemy was merely a system of morals veiled in symbols. Neither was right, but neither was wholly wrong. Alchemy, like yoga, does include certain practices akin to hypnosis; but this part of alchemical technique is applied by the alchemist to himself, and throughout his use of it, he retains self-conscious control of the process. The result is certainly the attainment of those qualities of character discussed by Hitchcock - or rather part of the result is the *expression* of those qualities in their highest and best terms. This, however, is made possible by a transformation which is more than an ordinary "moral awakening." This is a bodily transformation, which makes of the alchemist virtually a member of a new species, *beyond man*, as man is beyond the lower animals, and possessed of powers which go far beyond those of the average human being, including extraordinary control of the molecular and atomic structure of "matter," so-called.

Finally, remember that in alchemy, equilibrium is the basis of the work. All three principles are required. None is to be utterly abandoned, as those believe who tell us we must get rid of body (Salt) and dissipate completely the cohesive virtue of Tamas. Our alchemical Mercury must be perfectly *balanced* with our alchemical Salt, so that the latter is an adequate and useful embodiment of the former. In other words, the power of subconsciousness must be so adapted by the work of self-consciousness (Sulfur) that subconsciousness will give itself to the building and maintenance of suitable vehicles for the expression, here on earth, of superconscious powers.

The right performance of this work requires a thorough knowledge of the properties of what alchemists call "elements," and yogis, "tattvas." We shall begin our instruction on this in the next lesson, which will be devoted to THE ELEMENT OF FIRE.

V
THE ELEMENT OF FIRE

*A*lchemy is a philosophy of fire, a science of fire, and an art which consists mainly in the direction of fire. By Qabalah and Tarot we may unlock the secret meaning of alchemical writings and symbols, but we cannot use the keys until we have examined the locks. We shall begin this lesson, therefore, with quotations from the alchemists concerning the element of fire.

Paracelsus says,

> First and chiefly, the principle subject of this Art is fire, which always exists in one and the same property and mode of operation, nor can it receive its life from anything else. It possesses, therefore, a state and power, common to all fires which lie hid in secret, of vivifying. The fire in the furnace may be compared to the sun. It heats the furnace and the vessels, just as the sun heats the vast universe. For as nothing can be produced in the world without the sun, so also in this Art nothing can be produced without this simple fire. No operation can be completed without it. It is the Great Arcanum of Art, embracing all things which are comprised therein, neither can it be comprehended in anything else. It abides by itself, and needs nothing; but all others which stand in need of this can get fruition of it and have life from it. Know, then, that the ultimate and also the primal matter of everything is fire. This is, as it were, the key that unlocks the chest. It is this which makes manifest whatever is hidden in anything.
>
> By the element of fire all that is imperfect is destroyed and taken away, as for instance, the five metals, Mercury, Jupiter, Mars, Venus, and Saturn. On the other hand, the perfect metals, Sol and Luna, are not consumed in that same fire. They remain in the fire: and at the same time,

out of the other imperfect ones which are destroyed, they assume their own body and become visible to the eyes. For fire tests everything, and when the impure matter is separated the three pure substances are displayed. Fire separates that which is constant or fixed from that which is fugitive or volatile. Fire is the father or active principle of separation. Whatsoever pertains to separation belongs to the science of Alchemy. It teaches how to extract, coagulate, and separate every substance in its peculiar vessel. Fire contains within itself the whole of Alchemy by its native power to tinge, graduate, and fix, which is, as it were, born with it and impressed upon it.

Nundinus writes: "The fire which includes all our chemical processes is threefold: the fiery element of the air, of water, and of earth. This is *all* our magistery requires." Bondinus declares: "Our stone is fire, and has been generated in fire, without, however, being consumed by fire." According to Medales, "The fire of the sages may be extracted from all things, and is called the Quintessence. It is of earth, water, air, and fire."

Basil Valentine hides the secret in plain sight, thus:

> Our fire is a *common* fire, and our furnace is a *common* furnace. The fire of a spirit-lamp is useless for our purpose, nor is there any profit in horse dung, nor in the other kinds of heat in the providing of which so much expense is incurred. Neither do we want many kinds of furnaces. Only our threefold furnace affords facilities for properly regulating the heat of the fire. Our furnace is cheap, our fire is cheap, and our material is cheap. He who has the material will also find a furnace in which to prepare it, just as he who has flour will not be at a loss for an oven in which it may be baked.

Thomas Vaughan writes:

> Fire, notwithstanding the diversities of it in this sublunary kitchen of the elements, is but one thing from one root.

The effects of it are various, according to the distance and nature of the subject wherein it resides, for that makes it vital or violent. It sleeps in most things – as in flints, where it is silent and visible. It is a kind of *perdue*, lies close like a spider in the cabinet of his web, to surprise all that comes within his lines. He never appears without his prey in his foot; where he finds aught that's combustible, there he discovers himself, for – if we speak properly – he is not generated by manifested. There is nothing in the world generated without fire. This fire is at the root and about the root – I mean about the centre – of all things, both visible and invisible. It is in water, earth and air; it is in minerals, herbs, and beasts; it is in men, stars, and angels; but originally it is in God Himself, for He is the fountain of heat and fire, and from Him it is derived to the rest of the creatures in a certain stream or sunshine. Now, the magicians afford us but two notions whereby we may know their fire: it is, as they describe it, moist and invisible. Hence have they called it the horse's belly and horse dung; but this is only by way of analogy, for there is in horse dung a moist heat but no fire that is visible. Now then, let us compare the common Vulcan with this philosophical Vesta, that we may see wherein they are different. First of all then, the philosopher's fire is moist, and truly so is that of the kitchen too. We see that flames contract and extended themselves - now they are short, now they are long, which cannot be without moisture to maintain the flux and continuity of their parts. But the common fire is excessively hot, but moist in a far inferior degree, and therefore destructive, for it preys on the moisture of other things. On the contrary, the warmth and moisture of the magical agent are equal; the one temperates and satisfies the other: it is a humid, tepid fire, or, as we commonly express ourselves, blood-warm. This is their first and greatest difference in relation to our desired effect; we will now consider their second. The kitchen fire, as all know, is visible; but the philosopher's fire is invisible and therefore no kitchen fire. This Almadir expressly tells us in these words: "Our Work," saith he, "can be performed by nothing but by the invisible beams of our fire." And again,

"Our fire is a corrosive fire, which brings a cloud about our glass or vessel, in which cloud the beams of our fire are hidden." To be short, the philosophers call this agent their bath, because it is moist, as baths are; but in very truth is no kind of bath, neither of the sea nor of dew, but a most subtle fire and purely natural, but the excitation of it is artificial. (Condensed from *Lumen de Lumine*)

Boehme says:

When life and movement appears, which previously existed not, a principle is present. Fire is a principle with its property, and light is also a principle with its property, for it is generated from fire, and yet is not the fire's property. It has also its own life in itself, but fire is cause thereof. All sense, and whatever is to come to anything, must have fire. There springs nothing out of the earth without the essence of fire. It is a cause of all the three principles, and of all that can be named.

Many alchemical works quote from the *Chaldean Oracles*, a collection of Neo-Platonic fragments often attributed to Zoroaster, who probably had nothing to do with their composition. Their substance is practically the same as the teaching of Porphyry, in whose writings there is the following:

There is above the Celestial Lights an Incorruptible Flame always sparkling; the spring of life, the formation of all beings, the original of all things. This Flame produceth all things, and nothing perisheth but what it consumeth. It maketh itself known by itself. This Fire cannot be contained in any place; it is without body and without matter. It encompasseth the heavens.

The heart should not fear to approach this adorable Fire, or to be touched by it; it will never be consumed by this sweet Fire, whose mild and tranquil heat maketh the binding, the harmony, and the duration of the world. Nothing subsisteth but by this Fire, which is God Himself. All is full of God, and God is in all.

This universal fire of the alchemists is the same as the Agni or Tejas of Hindu Philosophy. Hindu Scriptures declare that Agni is the supreme deity, and attribute to him the powers of all the other gods of the pantheon. They represent him as a young ram, carrying a notched banner, inscribed with a swastika. This is precisely what is shown on the medals used by the Roman Church to represent Christ as the Lamb of God, or Agnus Dei. The only difference is that instead of the swastika, the banner bears a cross of equal arms. (See illustration, Agnus Dei, in *Webster's New International Dictionary.*)

In our interpretation of the Rosicrucian pamphlets, *Fama Fraternitatis* and *Confessio Fraternitatis*, we have shown how this peculiar symbolism of the young ram, or lamb, is employed to indicate the true nature of the Founder of the Rosicrucian Order, "Our Brother and Father, C.R." He represents the spiritual source of the higher consciousness attained in the alchemical Great Work, or by the practice of Yoga. He is what the *Book of Tokens* calls, "The circle of eternal flame, self-fed," and he is also a representation of the true alchemical fire.

Thus the quotation from Paracelsus tells us that the secret fire of the alchemists is the very life of the alchemical Art itself, and goes on to say that this hidden fire possesses the power of vivifying. The furnace he mentions is the athanor, which we have explained as being the human organism, itself produced from the "Essence of Fire," (אֶת הַנּוּר, *Ath Ha-Nour*). Observe, too, that he calls it a "simple" fire, meaning thereby that it is one without a second, a fire unmixed with anything whatsoever. The rest of the first paragraph from his writings is almost a paraphrase of the quotation from Porphyry. It plainly indicates that the secret fire is by no means to be confused with that which is manifest in ordinary combustion.

His remarks about the effect of fire on metals are to be understood as referring to the secret metals, or centers in the nervous system. Note that Sol and Luna, or Gold and Silver, are not destroyed by the secret fire. In the alchemical operation, the powers of all the other centers are transmuted into the powers of the "Sun" and "Moon." But here let it be remembered that the other *centers* are not destroyed. Their essential activities are raised, or sublimated, so that they all contribute to the perfect manifestation of the alchemical Gold, or spiritual illumination.

Nundinus and Medales identify the secret fire of alchemy with the Stone and with the Quintessence. The Stone, אבן, *Ehben*, is by Qabalah the same as the Sun, or Gold, חמה, *Khammaw*. The Quintessence is the same as the *Akasha* of the Hindus and the *Aether* of the Greeks.

Basil Valentine, as I have said, hides the secret in plain sight, by the use of the adjective "common." Uninstructed readers would suppose from this that he meant ordinary fire. The real thought is this: The philosophical fire is a fire common to all things, a fire shared by all. So also is the alchemical furnace a common possession. Everybody has the fire and the furnace, and those who waste their time and substance in looking outside themselves for these things betray their ignorance of the alchemical doctrine. The furnace is threefold, according to the esoteric division of the human personality into Body or alchemical Salt, Soul or alchemical Sulfur, and Spirit or alchemical Mercury.

Thomas Vaughan develops Valentine's doctrine that the fire is a *common* fire in several examples. He is careful to say, "He is not generated but manifested." This, of course, is common knowledge today. We do not generate any of the forces that modern invention utilizes in so many wonderful ways. We simply provide suitable conditions for the manifestation of those forces. Vaughan, furthermore, is confirmed by present-day science when he declares that the secret fire "is in water, earth and air; in minerals, herbs and beasts; in men, stars and angels." Recently some of the most important figures in the scientific world have also shown a disposition to agree also that this fire is, as Vaughan says, "originally in God Himself." It will be no new thing to readers familiar with other publications of the School of Ageless Wisdom to think of this magical agent as an influx of power which may properly be called "a certain stream or sunshine." Without any metaphor whatever, the alchemical fire *is* the essence of the radiant energy of the Sun, and this also is the substance of all things whatsoever.

It is moist, or like water, because it flows in streams, forms itself into whirlpools, collects like water in suitable reservoirs, has currents which may be charged almost as definitely as those of the sea, and forms itself into waves. At the same time, in itself it is invisible. We see its effects, but the energy itself remains hidden from us.

Vaughan's second quotation from Almadir deserves comment. The fire is said to be corrosive because it does actually "eat away by degrees." The glass or vessel is the auric egg. The cloud is the Physical body, which, according to certain esoteric doctrines is formed inside the auric egg by the action of the vital fire. This body is the veil which hides the beams of the secret fire.

The Hebrew word for fire is שׁאֵ, Ash. The same letters, with different vowel points, form the word שׁאִ, Ish, signifying entity. They are also the letters which spell the Aramaic noun שׁאֻ, Osh, a foundation. To the first letter, Aleph, the Ox, Qabalists attribute *Ruach*, the Life Breath, and this undifferentiated Life Breaththey call "Fiery or Scintillating Intelligence." The second letter is Shin, the Tooth, which is itself the letter of Fire, and the sign of the "Perpetual Intelligence." Furthermore, in Qabalah Shin is called the "Holy Letter" because its number is three hundred, is also the number of the words רוח אלהים, *Ruach Elohim*, Life Breathof the Creative Powers. Thus the two Hebrew letters which represent their noun for fire and both symbols for a fiery power, and symbols also of the Life Breath. They are likewise the first and last of the three "mother letters."

The alchemist's fire actually is Ruach, the all-pervading Life-Breath. Its primary manifestation is shown in the Tarot as the Fool, which represents the Life Breath as about to descend into the abyss of manifestation. This is true even in those ancient versions of this Key, which show a man about to fall into the open mouth of a crocodile. For the crocodile represents the lower nature, typified in our version of the Key by the depth which opens at the feet of the Fool. The fire of the alchemist, when it has entered into the abyss of manifestation, passes through all the transformations typified by the numbered Keys of Tarot following the Zero card, until it completes the circle of its activities in the resurrection typified by Key Twenty, attributed to the letter Shin.

The scene pictured in Key Twenty is the *anastasis*, or "rising again," usually called "resurrection" in the New Testament. Here we should be careful to remember that this is an esoteric term, especially in the four Gospels. There is reason to believe that it was misunderstood almost from the beginning of the public teaching of the Gnostic doctrine veiled in the exoteric letter of Christianity. In that doctrine the "dead" are those who are caught in the world's illusion, "dead in trespasses and sins." This point is made very clear by Ouspensky in his recent book, *A New Model of the Universe*. He says:

> In St. John's Gospel the idea of 'new birth' is introduced in explanation of the principles of esotericism.

Except a man be born again, he cannot see the kingdom of God. (*John* 3:3)

Then follows the idea of resurrection, resuscitation. Life without the idea of esotericism is regarded as death.

For as the Father raiseth up the dead, and quickeneth them; even so the Son quickeneth whom he will. (*John* 5:21)

Verily, Verily, I say unto you, the hour is coming, and now is, when the dead shall hear the voice of the Son of God; and they that hear shall live...

Marvel not at this; for the hour is coming, in the which all that are in the graves shall hear his voice. (*John* 5:25 and 28)

Verily, Verily, I say unto you, if a man shall keep my saying, he shall never see death. (*John* 8:51)

These last passages are certainly interpreted wrongly in existing pseudo-Christian teachings. 'These that are in the graves' does not mean dead people who are buried in the earth, but, on the contrary, those who are living in the ordinary sense, but dead from the point of view of esotericism...

The comparison of people with sepulchres or graves is met with several times in St. Mathew and St. Luke:

Woe unto you, scribed and Pharisees, hypocrites! For ye are like unto whited sepulchres, which indeed appear beautiful outward, but are within full of dead men's bones, and of all uncleanness (*Matt.* 23:27)

Woe unto you, scribes and Pharisees, hypocrites! For ye are as graves which appear not, and the men that walk over them are not aware of them (Luke 11:44).

The same idea is developed further in Revelations. Esotericism gives life. In the esoteric circle there is no death. (*A New Model of the Universe*, p181)

Now, the word *anastasis*, according to the Greek values of letters, is equivalent in number to the word *techne*, art, craft, skill, whence we derive our English word technic. The "rising again" is NOT a natural process. Thus Vaughan says that the magical agent is "subtle fire and purely natural, *but the excitation of it is artificial*." The same idea recurs again and again in esoteric writing. We are told that there is a force tremendously powerful, but man must direct it. Eliphas Levi goes so far as to say it is the burning body of the Holy Ghost. Yet he says that it is the devil of esoteric dogmatism, and the blind force which souls must conquer, if they would be freed from the chains of earth.

In other words, the alchemical fire must be first of all known, and then controlled. It will not, as many have imagined, change the present human race into supermen by any process of natural evolution. We may look forward to a day when the earth is governed and inhabited by none but Masters of Wisdom, but when that day comes, it will be because men and women have themselves taken in hand the direction of the alchemical fire. Not without reason is this work called The Great Art.

The Aramaic word for fire is נור, Noor. This is the word which we have already noticed in connection with את ה-נור, *Ath Ha-Noor*, athanor. It also appears in the word מנורה, *Menorah*, a candlestick, which is the same by numeration (301) as אש, *Ash*, fire. נור by its letters gives further indications as to the nature of the secret fire.

The first letter is Nun, to which the sign Scorpio, governing the organs of sex, is attributed in Qabalah. The second letter is Vau, to which is attributed the sign complementary and opposite to Scorpio, the sign Taurus, ruling the throat. The third letter is Resh, to which the Sun is attributed.

Now, in Scorpio Mars is the ruling planet, and Uranus (the Fool in Tarot) is exalted in that sign. In Taurus, Venus is the ruling planet, and the Moon is exalted, these two being represented in Tarot by the Empress and the High Priestess respectively. The Sun, symbolized by Key Nineteen, is the ruler of the heart and spinal cord, through the heart center and the sign Leo, and is exalted in the sign Aries, ruled by Mars, governing the head and brain.

Thus in the one word נור a Qabalist would find references to the Sun, Moon, Venus, and Mars, and to the bodily areas of the brain, throat, and ears, heart and spinal cord, and organs of sex. The corresponding tarot Keys are 19 (Sun Center), 2 (Moon Center), 3 (Throat Center), 16 (Mars Center), 4 (Head and Brain), 5 (Throat and Ears), 8 (Heart and Spinal Cord), 13 (Sex Organs).

These are valuable clues. For in the actual Hermetic practice, the centers and areas just named are of primary importance. The secret fire of the philosophers is, as Valentine asserts, a *common* fire, present everywhere, and available to all men. It is also the essential vital principle in all forms of manifestation whatsoever. At the same time, it has certain special types of manifestation which are the ones the alchemist employs in the technical operations of the Great Art. These are the forms of the secret fire which are at work in the parts of the human body indicated by our analysis of the word נור.

Hence alchemy must remain today, as it has in the past, more or less a secret doctrine. A full, detailed explanation of certain facts about the secret fire cannot be made, even if one desired to make it, without incurring severe penalties. Greater freedom in the explanation and discussion of the facts of sex is possible then heretofore, but there still exist legal restrictions to plain speaking, and every effort to change these restrictions is met with vigorous opposition from the organized, influential powers to whose interest it is to maintain popular ignorance.

Let it be said once more, however, that the alchemical process is not concerned with any sort of jugglery with the sex-function. Our inability to discuss the matter freely arises from the fact that neither the physiology nor psychology of that function may be accurately described or defined in any work intended, as this is, for general circulation.

As to the practice, even though there were no restrictions such as we have just mentioned, only the most general indications can be given. Consider only the centers and organs involved. They are the most delicate, and the most important in the human organism. It is extremely dangerous to try any tricks with them. Even under the personal guidance of a competent instructor, who knows every detail of the alchemical process, there is some degree of danger. Without such guidance a rash experimenter runs very real and very terrible risks.

For the secret fire is indeed a corrosive flame, and when it is intensified by the practical operations of the Great Art, it is more than strong enough to destroy like lightning, unless proper precautions be taken.

In Tarot, fire is represented primarily by the letter Shin and Key Twenty. This Key gives the most direct intimations concerning the nature and use of the secret fire. Three other Keys are also connected with fire, because they represented the three fiery signs of the zodiac, Aries, Leo and Sagittarius. The corresponding Keys are Four, The Emperor; Eight, Strength; and Fourteen, Temperance.

Key Twenty, Judgment, illustrates the threefold manifestation of the One Fire, mentioned in the quotation from Nundinus, by the symbolism of the three figures rising from the coffins of stone. These figures may be interpreted as representing the same idea as that which is typified by the three sides of the right-angled triangle, discussed in Lesson Three. The man is Osiris, the Father. The woman is Isis, the Mother. Between them is Horus, the child, who is the Son, "one with the Father."

The angel overhead, who is, by the implications of the scene and of the title of the Key, the archangel Gabriel. But according to the Qabalah, Gabriel is the angel of water. Here there seems to be a contradiction, until we remember the alchemists' own explicit declaration that they "burn with water," and call to mind also the several hints given by authors quoted in this lesson, to the effect that there is a fluidic quality about their secret fire.

The icy peaks or glaciers in the background of the 20th Key, and the expanse of water supporting the coffins, are symbols of this fluidic fire. The coffins themselves are made of stone, and they float upon the sea, to intimate that the solid forms of the mineral kingdom are really supported by the universal fluidic energy. The human figures have been enclosed in the coffins, but are now emerging. Here is the idea that the potencies of human consciousness are present even in mineral forms. To this the passage of Scripture refers which declares that God is able out of stones to raise up children unto Abraham.

The letter Shin, corresponding to this Key and to fire, is, as has been explained, related by its number to the words *Ruach Elohim*, Life Breathof the Creative Powers. Three hundred is the extension of twenty-four (the sum of the numbers from zero to twenty-four inclusive.) Thus three hundred represents the full development of the idea symbolized in Revelations by the twenty-four thrones of the Elders. Twenty-four itself is the number of the Hebrew word גויה, *Geviyeh*, meaning "substance," or "body." Thus here is a hint that the secret fire is simply the extended manifestation of that same reality which gives body to all things, or is the substance of everything. Hence in the diagram of the Egyptian triangle on page 55 of Lesson Three, you will notice that the first space in the line attributed to Isis is that assigned to the element of fire. Similarly, in Qabalah, the first letter of the Tetragrammaton, יהוה, is said to stand for the same element. This letter is I or Yod, and Qabalists declare that among the Ten Sephiroth, Yod belongs to חכמה, *Chokmah*, Wisdom, the second aspect of the Life Power. This again connects with the idea of fire, because Chokmah is said to be the "Root of Fire." Chokmah, again, is the seat of חיה, *Chaiah*, the Life Force, and is also the Sphere of Masloth, "the highways of the stars."

Complicated as these Qabalisms may appear to some readers of these pages, they are clues to the alchemical mystery. In this connection we must remember the words of Paracelsus, in the second chapter of his book, *The Tincture of the Philosophers*:

> Now, if you do not understand the use of the Qabalists and the old astronomers, you are not born by God for the Spagyric Art, or chosen by Nature for the work of Vulcan, or created to open your mouth concerning alchemical arts.

"Spagyric Art" is a name for alchemy, derived from two Greek roots, one meaning "to separate," the other, "to assemble." Thus the whole art has been summed up in two Latin words, *Solve*, to dissolve, and *Coagula*, to thicken; and it is said to consist in the volatilization of the fixed and the fixation of the volatile.

The process of assimilation, for example, is a phase of the alchemical process. It begins by the destruction of the solid forms of food, and their gradual volatilization (by mechanical and chemical activities in the alimentary canal and stomach), up to the point where the "Virgin's Milk" is taken up by the lacteals in the small intestine. From that point fixation begins, as the energy assimilated is built into the structure of the body. This on the Physical plane.

On the mental plane, analysis of experience leads to the discovery of the forces, laws, and principles behind what affects our senses. This analysis is performed with the help of Mercury, or self-consciousness, and the Magician in Tarot is a picture of the process. It is followed by the synthesis of the principles, laws, and forces discovered by analysis. New combinations are made through the operation of creative imagination, as symbolized by the Empress. Thus man is enabled to introduce into the operations of nature new manifestations of her own laws, which she cannot produce except through human agency.

Knowledge of the "use," that is, of the methods, of the Qabalah and of the old astronomy, or astrology, is indispensable to would-be alchemists, because long ago the fundamental laws of mental and physical analysis and synthesis were found out by the Inner School, and embodied in the symbolisms of astrology and Hebrew Wisdom.

The Qabalah is fundamentally a mathematical system, and its root ideas are developed through number and geometry. All the intricacies of Qabalistic geometry are derived from the following simple problem, with which Euclid began his famous works. It is the method for constructing an equilateral triangle, as follows:

Describe a circle. With unaltered compasses describe a second circle, using any point on the circumference of the first circle as the center of the second. The space enclosed by the intersecting lines of the two circles is called a Vesica Piscis. It is a key to many secrets of architecture, Free Masonry, and Qabalah. Connect the upper point of the Vesica with the centers of the two circles by straight lines, and the centers of the two circles by another straight line. The three straight lines will form the equilateral triangle which is the alchemical symbol for the element of fire.

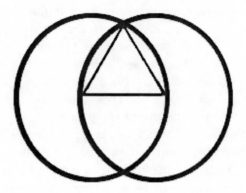

The two circles forming the Vesica Piscis are an ancient symbol of the threefold nature of Reality, because the two arcs of the Vesica are each two-sixths of a circle, and each of the circles outside the Vesica has, besides that part of it which is included in the Vesica, a remaining arc of two-sixths. The triangle also definitely indicates the number three. So does the numeral value of the letter Shin, three hundred, because three hundred may be Qabalistically reduced to three.

 The form of this letter, shown in the margin, is also immediately suggestive of the number three. So also, as you have seen, is the symbolism of the 20th Tarot Key. The number three is also hidden in the number of this Key, Twenty, because the sum of the numbers from one to twenty is two hundred and ten, and the digits of two hundred and ten add to three.

Key Four, The Emperor, illustrates the activity of the alchemical fire in the head of man, in the faculty of vision, and in the power of reason. Through the connection of this Key with the letter Heh, the symbolism is all related to the sign Aries.

Now, Aries is typified as a young ram, or lamb, called טלה, *Taleh*, in Hebrew. This word is numbered forty-four, and is equivalent to דם, *Dam*, Blood, to חול, *Khool*, Sand, and to להט, *Lahat*, Flame and Magic. The connection between Aries and the Hindu fire-god Agni is obvious. And in another lesson of this series we have considered the correspondences between blood, sand, and flame. Just now, what I would emphasize is the idea of rulership, or control, intimated by the title of Key Four. The alchemical fire is the fire of reason. It is the fiery energy that is at work in the brain. It is the force which takes form in physical and mental vision. It is the power whereby order is established throughout the manifested universe. This power, when we recognize it, and permit it to work without interference through us, is a magic power. In itself it is the power of composing, framing, or constituting worlds. Thus when it finds expression through a properly prepared human brain it enables the possessor of that brain to see things as they really are, and brings about so perfect a personal manifestation of reason that all details of that person's life are rightly ordered.

Key Eight, Strength, is connected with the sign Leo, through its attribution to the letter Teth. Some of the profound alchemical significance of this Key has been touched upon elsewhere in this course. This Key also has links of connection with the central mystery of Free Masonry, which has to do with the raising of the dead body of Hiram Abiff, by means of the "strong grip of the lion's paw." In the Masonic legend, we are told that the body was at an advanced stage of putrefaction, which is a direct reference to the alchemical doctrine that the materials of the Great Work must be utterly decomposed before they can be raised, or sublimated. In this connection, remember that אביו חורם, the Hebrew spelling of *Hiram Abiff*, is the number two hundred seventy-three, and this is the number also of אבן מאסו הבונים, *Ehben Masu Ha-Bonim*,

The Stone which the Builders rejected. Careful consideration of these three words may also lead some of my Masonic readers to discover a clue to the true significance of the "substitute" for the Lost Word, for the syllables of the substitute are concealed in these three words.

It is also interesting to note that the Temple which was nearing completion when Hiram Abiff was killed was situated on Mount Moriah. The bearing of this on our present study is that the words הר המוריה, *Ha-Moriyah Har*, Mount Moriah, add up to four hundred seventy-one, which is the spelling of the word אש, Ash, Fire, "in plenitude," thus: אלף שין. The implication of this Qabalism is that the "Temple" is built upon a foundation of fire. This is further borne out by the fact that מוריה, *Moriah*, means "seen of Yah," or "Hill of vision," so that it is directly connected with the power of vision already noticed in connection with Key Four. And to confirm this, the Hebrew for "temples," היכלות, *haikaluth*, is also the number four hundred and seventy-one.

Here is another point. The Aramaic word נור, Nour, written in its plenitude, is נון-וו-ריש, and totals six hundred and twenty-eight. Six hundred and twenty-eight is 4 x 157, and four hundred and seventy-one, the value of שי-אלף, or אש in plenitude, is 3 x 157. Thus there is a relation between the numbers representing these two words. One hundred and fifty-seven is the number of the words in the phrase דמדומי חמה, the setting of the sun, and of the words זקן, *zaqan*, the beard, מופלא, *mowpelah*, Occult, miraculous, hidden (applied to Kether, the Crown, in Qabalah), and נקבה, *neqebeh*, female. The "beard" is regarded by many Qabalists as being a euphemism for the masculine aspect of the creative power, and the word

Neqebeh, Female, is directly derived from a root meaning "that which is pierced." Thus these two words correspond more or less to the ideas represented by the Hindu lingam and yoni. The idea suggested is that the secret fire is both male and female, and this is exactly what is taught by the Hindus when they say that the secret fire used in Yoga is both solar and lunar, active and passive, male and female.

Key Fourteen, Temperance, corresponds to the letter Samekh, which has the value sixty. This is the value of the word בחן, *bachan*, to try or test, applied especially to metals, and implying that the trial is by fire. Here students of our writings on Qabalah will remember that the path of intelligence attributed to the letter Samekh is called "Intelligence of Probation or Trial." Again, the number sixty is the number of the word כלי, *keliy*, a vessel, something prepared, apparatus. It refers to the secret vessels of alchemy, and these are symbolized in Key Fourteen by the vase which the angel holds, and from which water is poured upon the head of a lion. In older exoteric versions of this Key there are two vases, one in each hand of the angel, who pours a triple stream from cup to cup, without spilling a drop. This is also excellent symbolism, if not quite so specific as that of the esoteric Tarot which is the basis of the design issued by us.

The zodiacal sign Sagittarius, corresponding to Key Fourteen, is called קשת, *qesheth*, meaning primarily "bow," and often used to designate the rainbow, but also signifying "bowman" or "archer." This word has a particular significance in Qabalah, because it is composed of the letters assigned to the three paths connecting Malkuth, the Kingdom, with the higher Sephiroth on the Tree of Life.

The number of קשת, *qesheth*, is eight hundred, and this is the value of the letter Peh when it comes at the end

of a word. Peh is the letter of Mars, and is connected with
the Mars center in the body. This is the center which in-
nervates the reproductive organs, and corresponds to the
Svadistthana Chakra of the yogis. This center is said to be
the seat of the Apas Tattva in the yoga doctrine, and since
this is the Tattva of Water, we have here once more the
apparent confusion of fire and water which we noticed in
connection with the angel Gabriel. And it is to be noticed
that in the 14th Key water is a prominent symbol. So, also,
in Key Sixteen of Tarot, which represents the Mars-force,
there are storm clouds, so that the implication is that the
fiery force there shown destroying the tower is somehow
connected with water.

Again, the number eight hundred is the number of
שרש, *shoresh*, a root, indicating that whatever occult significance there may be in the word קשת, *qesheth*, may be
expected to lead us to a better understanding of that which
is the root, or fundamental, of all the forms of growth and
development.

Years of familiarity with this material have undoubtedly made it easier for me to trace the connections between these Qabalistic clues to the occult doctrine of the
secret fire. Just as an Apache tracker can discern marks
on a trail which would be of no significance to the eyes of
the average passer-by, so does one who has devoted years
to making himself acquainted with the symbolic language
of the Qabalah see plain indications when another will see
nothing at all.

Nevertheless, I believe that when the clues are brought
together, as they are in these lessons, any person who is really in earnest in his desire to penetrate the veil of symbolism behind which the secrets of the Hermetic Art are hidden will be able, if he thinks through what is given here, to
discover the truth of the matter.

It must always be remembered, however, that the most

important secrets of Hermetic Science *cannot* be put into ordinary language. We would tell them, if telling were possible, but there are no words in any human language which can communicate this knowledge. There are words, and other forms of symbolic expression such as Tarot, which, if meditated upon, will bring the student's mind to the point where he can know for himself. Then all the words and symbols will take on a new meaning for him. He will understand that there is truly a magical language, and that it does serve, like all language, to aid communication *between those who understand it.*

The study of Tarot and Qabalah are preparations for this understanding. The mental effort expended in such study has its inevitable physical results. It does actually modify the structure of the brain. It makes one more and more receptive. Thus I have felt it necessary to include a considerable number of Qabalisms in this lesson, to the end that earnest students may be given the necessary materials for the exercise of mental functions which no other kind of thinking can call into play.

In recent years much nonsense has been written about the verbal "juggling" of the technical Qabalah. As Muraskin says, in his introduction to Harry Waton's valuable work, *The Philosophy of the Kabbalah*, "Far from being arbitrary word juggling, the technical Kabbalah constitutes a well ordered mathematical system, in no wise inferior to our own system of symbolic logic." Furthermore, even juggling requires and develops dexterity, so that if nothing further were to be brought about by the use of this technique of permutation, transposition, and numerical valuation of the letters in Hebrew words, it would be worth doing for the sake of the mental flexibility and agility which it certainly does result in.

What really happens, however, is an unusual training of the power of association. The numeral correspondences between words are merely signals, so to say, which arrest our attention. On the surface, the words have no obvious relation to each other; but when we notice that they have the same number, we begin to look for the connecting links between them. And it is in the pursuit of these chains of association that we unfold the hidden knowledge.

For example, אחד, *achad*, Unity and אהבה, *ahebah*, Love, both correspond to the number 13, and this is a fairly obvious relation that almost any one can see. But what is meant by the fact that איב, *ayab*, Hate, is also numbered thirteen? Hate repels, and love attracts. Surely these are exact opposites. But are they? What more surely attaches our minds to another than to hate him? Is there any force more binding than thorough aversion? Recent developments in analytical psychology have shown conclusively that hate and love are but opposite sides of the same shield. Thus this one example of technical Qabalah is also an example of the transcendental logic which Ouspensky expresses thus: Everything is both A and Not-A at one and the same time. (*Tertium Organum*)

Paracelsus understood the Hermetic Science and was a great adept in the Hermetic Art. If, then, you are disposed to chafe a little at the Qabalisms in this lesson, remember his words, quoted on page 112. The only way you can "understand the use of the Qabalists" is by considering examples of their method. At first you may be like a child who is learning to read. You may be so occupied with your attempts to pronounce single words that the story told by them will make no impression upon you. Persist, and the time will come when the story will be all that you notice, because practice has made easy the reading of the symbols in which it is told.

Summing up this lesson, then, the main points are as follows:

1. The fire of the alchemists is closely related to their First Matter, for it is, as Paracelsus tells us, "the principal subject of this Art."

2. It is not the ordinary fire of combustion, but a hidden, occult force which is characterized by its power of vivifying.

3. Some call it a "common" fire, meaning that it is common to all things.

4. It is identical with the STONE.

5. It is one thing, from one root.

6. In many respects it resembles a fluid, and is often disguised by alchemical writers under the name "Water."

7. It is silent and invisible.

8. It is not generated but manifested.

9. It is purely natural, but the excitation of it is artificial.

10. This fire, according to Boehme, is the root of light, which is generated from it.

11. It is the cause of the three principles, and of all that can be named.

12. It is God Himself.

13. It is the power which forms the physical body of man.

14. It is identical with *Ruach*, the Life Breath.

15. It is the power which raises the "dead" (in the esoteric sense), as shown in Key Twenty of Tarot.

16. The means whereby this result is accomplished is the Great Work of alchemy.

17. In the human body, where it becomes the subject of the alchemical operation, this fire is particularly connected with the nerve centers and organs of reproduction. It is also active in certain other centers. (See page 109)

18. This fire is represented by the first letter of the Tetra-grammaton, יהוה, consequently it is identical with the Life Force in the human organism, because the first letter of יהוה is also attributed to Chokmah, the second aspect of Reality, and to Chokmah the Qabalah assigns חיה, *Chaiah*, the Life Force.

19. This Life Force is identical with the radiant energy which emanates from suns, and which is the motive power of all the heavenly bodies.

A careful consideration of these points, and equally careful rereading of this lesson should serve to plant deep in your subconsciousness the seed-thoughts of the alchemical doctrine of fire. Give these seed-ideas time to germinate. Nobody learns alchemy altogether from books. The written word is but the means to awaken the subconscious process of deduction. This lesson provides you with the essence of what the sages have written concerning their fire. Your inner consciousness will develop their doctrine into the ripe fruit of understanding and realization.

In the next lesson we shall consider the alchemical doctrine concerning the element of water.

VI
THE ELEMENT OF WATER

Water, in the alchemical doctrine, is the element which contains the potencies of all forms of manifestation. Thus it is often called the "Mother," and in the account of creation in the Book of Genesis, it is designated as the first element, or matter, of the world. There we read: "The Life Breath of the Creative Powers brooded upon the face of the abyss of waters," and the consequence of this brooding was the whole creation. Yet this alchemical water is by no means our common water. This you will see for yourself, after reading the following quotations from the writings of various alchemists.

In the *Turba Philosophorum* it is said: "The ignorant, when they hear us name water, think it is water of the clouds; but, if they understood our books, they would know it to be a permanent or fixed water, which without its Sulfur - to which it hath been united - cannot be permanent."

Thomas Vaughan declares: "Our subject is no common water, but a thick, slimy, fat earth. This earth must be dissolved in water, and that water must be coagulated again into earth." (In this short statement is to be found one of the clearest and most accurate descriptions of the actual material used in alchemy, and of the process by which it is manipulated.) Vaughan also writes: "Among visible things the water first shone forth; this was the fruitful mother of figurable things, the feminine in correspondence with the masculine of indwelling fire."

Sendivogius wrote: "Our water is a heavenly water, which wets not the hand, not that of the common man, but

123

almost, as it were, pluvial." The adjective "pluvial" means literally, "rainy," but the context denies that the alchemical water is the ordinary fluid which falls from the clouds. The meaning is that the alchemical water descends in drops. It is "heavenly," that is to say, metaphysical, yet it does assume a drop-like, or corpuscular, form.

Raymond Lully is even more specific in his indication that the alchemical water is not common water. "It hath the likeness of the sun and moon," he writes, "and in such water it hath appeared unto us." The sun is a "likeness," or presentation, of this water, and so is the moon. Here is a definite identification of the heavenly or celestial water with that current of energy whose flux and reflux is the agency of all manifestation, presented to the human eye in the actual forms of sun, moon, and stars.

Another alchemist tells us:

> As the world was generated out of that water, upon which the Spirit of God did move, all things proceeding from thence, both celestial and terrestrial, so this philosophical chaos is generated out of a certain water that is not common, not out of dew, nor air condensed in the caverns of the earth, nor artificially in the receiver; nor out of water drawn from the sea, fountains, pits, or rivers, but out of a certain tortured water, that hath suffered some alteration obvious to all, but known to few. This water hath in it all that is necessary for the perfection of the philosophical work, without any extrinsical addition.

In his *Mysterium*, Jacob Boehme says:

> When I behold the external water, I am forced to say, 'Here in the water below the firmament is also contained water from above the firmament.' But the firmament is the middle, and the link between time and eternity, so that neither one of them is the other. By means of the external eyes, or the eyes of this world, I see only the water below the firmament; but the water above the firmament is that which God in

Christ has instituted for the baptism of regeneration.

In the *Aurora* he writes:

> The water of life became separated from the water of death; but in such a way that in the time of this world they are linked together like body and soul. But the heaven, having been made from the middle-part of the water is like an abyss between the two, so that the conceivable water is a death, but the inconceivable one is the life.
>
> The water upon the earth is a degenerated and deadly being, like the earth herself. This material water, contained within the most external generation, has been separated from the inconceivable one.

Thomas Vaughan also says, in *Anthroposophia Theomagica*:

> I am now to speak of the Water. This is the first element we read of in Scripture, the most ancient of principles and the Mother of all things among visibles. Without the mediation of this, the Earth can receive no blessing at all, for moisture is the proper cause of mixture and fusion. The water hath several complexions (understand here 'Combinations in certain proportions') according to the several parts of the creature. Here below, and in the circumference of all things, it is volatile, crude, and raw. For this very cause Nature makes it no part of her provision, but she rectifies it first, exhaling it up with her heat, and thus condensing it into rains and dews, in which state she makes use of it for nourishment. Somewhere it is interior, vital, and celestial, exposed to the breath of the First Agent, and stirred with spiritual eternal winds. In this condition it is Nature's wanton— *Foemina Satacissima*, as one calls it. This is that Psyche of Apuleius, and the Fire of nature is her Cupid. He that hath seen them both in the same bed will confess that love rules all. But to speak something of our common, elemental Water. It is not altogether contemptible; there are hidden treasures in it, but so enchanted we cannot see them, for all that the chest is transparent. 'The congealed spirit of the Invisible Water is better than the whole earth,' saith the noble and learned

> Sendivogius. I do not advise the reader to take this phlegm to task, as if he would extract a Venus from the sea, but I wish him to study Water that he may know the Fire.

Finally, Paracelsus says:

> The first matter of minerals consists of water; and it comprises only Sulphur, Salt and Mercury. These minerals are that element's spirit and soul, containing in themselves all minerals, metals, gems, salts, and other things of that kind, like different seeds in a bag.

The chemical formula for ordinary water is H_2O, or two parts hydrogen and one part oxygen. Recently it has been discovered that there are two kinds of hydrogen atoms, one heavier than the other, and by isolating the heavy atoms it has been possible to make a "heavy" water which differs from ordinary water in several particulars. Plants and tadpoles are poisoned by it, and it seems to have certain other properties which are just now engaging the interest of research chemists. But even "heavy" water is a compound of hydrogen and oxygen.

Hydrogen, though not resembling the metals physically, is like metals in that it is electro-positive, and is the positive ion (H+) of all acids. Chemically, hydrogen is the typical monad, or universal element. Oxygen is eight-ninths, by weight, of ordinary water, and nearly one-half, by weight, of the rocks composing the earth's crust. Liquid oxygen is strongly magnetic. Thus even the ordinary water is a compound of elements having the characteristic qualities of the alchemical "sun" and "moon," for the former, like hydrogen, is electro-positive, and the latter, like liquid oxygen, is invariably distinguished as being magnetic.

These facts, brought to light by modern chemical research, confirm the alchemical dictum that water is the seed and root of all metals. Yet we must remember that alchemical water is not precisely the H_2O of chemistry. One key to its real nature is the oft-repeated declaration that it is a "heavenly" water which "does not wet the hand." It is metaphysical, or heavenly, in its inner nature, although it does give rise to phenomena which make their appearance on the physical plane.

The methods whereby the sages arrived at their knowledge were not the methods of the modern chemist. Yet their conclusions are in many particulars identical with those of modern chemistry, because their methods were really practical. Instead of observing chemical reactions in test tubes and retorts, they studied the forces of nature *directly*, utilizing a higher order of perception. Thus they perceived the existence of an all-pervading element which FLOWS, which has CURRENTS, which falls upon earth in a drop-like formation, and which presents itself to the physical eye as the sun and moon.

This element they symbolized by precisely the same figure as that which they used for fire – an equilateral triangle. But they turned the point of the triangle downward, as shown in the margin. By so doing they indicated that when it manifests as the element of water, the One Thing, or Single Force, moves, so to say, in a direction opposite to that which it takes when it manifests as the element of Fire.

Thus Paracelsus says: "Know, then, that the ultimate and also the primal matter of everything is fire. This is, as it were, the key that locks the chest. It is this which makes manifest whatever is hidden in anything." The fire is the One Thing mentioned in the *Emerald Tablet*. When it ascends from earth to heaven it is symbolized by the upright triangle, and by the various other emblems which have been discussed in the preceding lesson.

When this same force descends to earth it is represented by the triangle pointing downward. Thus we know, at the very beginning of this study, that the alchemical water is really that movement of the One Force which is mentioned in the *Emerald Tablet* when it is said: "Its power is integrating, if it be turned into earth." In other words, the alchemical water is the form-producing operation or aspect of the One Thing.

Thus we find that this element is represented by the second letter of the Tetragrammaton, יהוה. And in Qabalistic works we read: "Creation took place with the letter Heh (H)." and since we have seen elsewhere that the second letter of יהוה is also the symbol for the Qabalistic "world" or plane called בריאה, *Briah*, the Creative World, we may understand the metaphysical water of the alchemists as being the aspect assumed by the One Energy on the plane so named.

Here it is important to say that when we call the alchemical water "metaphysical," we do not by any means mean to imply that it is a mere intellectual abstraction. It is just as "real" as physical water, just as actual as a brick. Occultists use the term "metaphysical" in a special, and literal, sense. By this adjective they mean "existing *beyond* the range of physical sensation." In the Qabalistic philosophy which the alchemists adapted to their special purposes, the highest metaphysical reality is called אין, or No-Thing; אין סוף, *En Soph*, or the Limitless; and אור אין סוף, *En Soph Aur*, or Limitless Light. These are the names given to the One Reality prior to the beginning of a cycle of manifestation, and they are called "Veils of the Absolute" because Qabalists understand perfectly well that any description or definition of the Absolute must necessarily conceal, or veil, its real nature.

Yet it is always needful to remind ourselves that the Absolute of the Qabalists is *not* an abstraction. It is not the result of speculative philosophizing. It is a Reality which has been directly experienced by the sages, to whom it is something truly *known*, even though it is also something which remains ineffable because there are no human words to describe it.

Just below that aspect of the One Reality which is termed אין אסף אור, *En Soph Aur*, or Limitless Light, is the "octave" or "field" or "world" or "plane" of manifestation called Atziluth, the Archetypal World. This plane is related to the element of fire, and is attributed to the first letter of יהוה. It would be correct to say, then, that alchemical fire is the metaphysical substance of the archetypal world, and that alchemical water is the metaphysical substance of the creative world.

You have just seen that the symbol for alchemical water is identical with the symbol for alchemical fire, except that its direction is reversed. The identity of the alchemical water with alchemical fire is also declared by the alchemists themselves, who say, "Philosophers *burn* with water." So also Synesius, who writes: "I advise thee, my son, to make no account of other things; labour only for that water which *burns to blackness*, dissolves, and congeals." Elsewhere this same water is called "golden," which is to say, "solar," since Gold and Sun are equivalent in alchemy.

In the Hebrew alphabet, the Mother letter corresponding to water is מים, *Mem*. This is the letter represented in Tarot by the 12th Key, THE HANGED MAN. The name of the letter itself means water, and represents the equation $40+10+40 = 90$, which is the value of the letter name. As a character, מ, the letter has the value forty.

Beginning with this number, forty, we find that it is the value of the verb גזל, meaning primarily, "to cut off, to take away." Here we have a direct reference to what is implied in the alchemical idea that the element of water is the source of *form*, and that it is associated with the "creative letter," Heh. Since all things are manifestations of One Reality, besides which there is, or can be, nothing whatever, it follows that what seems to us to be the multiplication of forms is actually only a sub-division of the One into various *parts*. Thus the Hebrew verb ברא, which is the root of the word בריאה, *Briah*, the Creative World, means "to cut apart." This agrees with what has been said in Lesson Four (page 89) concerning the diversifying power of the Sephirah Binah.

Again, forty is the number of the word חבל, which, as a verb, means: 1) to wind together, to bind; 2) to pledge; 3) to wound, to damage, to destroy. As a noun it means: 1) pain, sorrow; 2) a cord, a rope; 3) a measuring line; 4) a snare. Compare the first of these meanings with the words of Vaughan, quoted on page 125: "Moisture is the proper cause of mixture and fusion." And since the creative process is a breaking up of the "still calm of Pure Being," there is a sense in which the original purity of the subsisting ONE is damaged or destroyed by the creative process. Thus we hear again and again that the One Life sacrifices Itself for the sake of manifestation. We hear, too, that limitation and measurement are inseparable from creation; that the world of appearances resulting from the creative process is a scene of pain and sorrow; and that this world is a delusion and a snare to those who misapprehend the meaning of its appearance.

A third Hebrew word corresponding to forty is חלב, which means 1) milk; 2) fatness; 3) superabundance; 4) the best part. Here we are reminded that what is called "Water" by some alchemists is termed "Virgin's Milk" by others. Again, fatness is a characteristic of alchemical water, according to the quotation from Thomas Vaughan on page 123. It is from the alchemical water that the wise derive all their supplies of substance for manifestation as external forms, and our quotation from Synesius (page 129) seems to indicate it as being the "best part," or most desirable thing.

A fourth correspondence to forty is the Hebrew idiom
יד יהוה *Yod Tetragrammaton*, which means literally "The
Hand of the Eternal," but really signifies the power (understand *formative* power) of the One Reality. Thus we
may understand that the alchemical water is actually the
agency, or power, whereby the One Reality projects Its creative energy into specific shapes or forms.

Turning now to the correspondences to ninety, the
number of the noun מים, Mem, the first is דומם, *Domem*,
"in silence." This is directly connected with the letter
Mem, which is said by Qabalists to be "mute, like water."

The second correspondence to ninety is יכין, *Jachin*,
the name of one of the pillars before the porch of Solomon's temple. This word, familiar to Free Masons, signifies, according to some, "firm one, strong one, patron." It
is interpreted in Masonry as meaning "He will establish,"
and thus has somewhat the same underlying significance
as יד יהוה, *Yod Tetragrammaton*, The Hand of the Eternal.
The noun is from a Semitic root meaning "Unity," and refers to the creative power of the One Thing.

A third correspondence to the number ninety is the
word מלך. As a verb it means "to administer, to reign, to
rule, to counsel." As a noun it means "king, ruler, prince."
Thus it conveys the idea or rulership, royalty, command,
and the like. For the alchemical water is actually the agency whereby the rule or administration of the Life Power
over all forms is established.

A fourth correspondence is to the proper name למך,
Lamech. This is important in Free Masonry also, since Lamech is the name of the Biblical character (Gen. 4.18)
who, according to Masonic tradition was the father of that
ancient Craft. In this connection it is interesting to note
that the Greek spelling of this name, as used in the New
Testament is ΛΑΜΕΧ = 676, which is the *square* of twenty-

six, the number indicated by the Divine Name יהוה, *Tetra-grammaton*. The literal meaning of the word is "powerful." The traditional connection of this name with Free Masonry, and the correspondence of its Greek equivalent to the number six hundred seventy-six are indications (however slight they may seem to a person unversed in the subtleties of the Qabalah) that the alchemical water is somehow related to all things having to do with creation and construction.

Now, Paracelsus says also:

> The first principle with God was the ultimate matter which he himself made to be the primal, just as a fruit which produces another fruit. It has seed; and this seed ranks as primal matter. Likewise, out of the ultimate matter of minerals the primal element was made, that is, it was made into seed, which seed is the element of water... So, then, the element of water is the mother, seed, and root of all minerals; and the Archaeus therein is he who disposes everything according to a definite order, so that each comes to its ultimate matter, which at length man receives as a sort of artificial primal matter; that is, where Nature ends, there the Art of man begins, for Nature's ultimate matter is man's primal matter. After such a wonderful method has God created water as the first matter of nature, so soft and weak a substance, yet from it as a fruit the most solid metal, stones, etc.- the very hardest from the very softest - and so that from the water fire should issue forth, beyond the grasp of man's intelligence, but not beyond the power of Nature.

The Archaeus is the Universal Agent, specialized in each individual thing, creature, and personality. By some it is understood to be identical with the *Anima Mundi*, or Soul of the World, and this *Anima Mundi*, which works at subconscious levels throughout Nature is that principle which maintains and directs the growth of living beings, sets all nature in motion, and is especially active in the development, growth and reproduction of all living beings. In this connection it might be well to read carefully the writings of Judge Troward, particularly *The Creative Process in the Individual*, *The Hidden Power*, and *The Law and the Word*, for of all modern writers, this author sets forth most clearly the nature of the *Anima Mundi*, and indicates how, and for what reasons, it must be carefully distinguished from the higher spiritual soul. In a word, the *Anima Mundi*, which Paracelsus declares to be the Archaeus in the primal water, is none other than the Maya-Shakti of the Hindu philosophers. As the power which gives shape and form to all things it is clearly the same as the finitising principle of the Thomistic philosophy, mentioned in connection with the Sephirah Binah on page 89 of Lesson Four.

Binah is the Sphere of Saturn, and Saturn is the astrological correspondence to the finitising principle. Saturn condenses, fixes, materializes, restricts. Thus Saturn corresponds to the alchemical idea of saltiness associated with the Great Sea of Binah. But just as "finitising" and "finishing" both come from the same Latin root, so Saturn, as the representative of that which establishes definite form, is also representative of that which brings things to completion. This is one of the reasons why Saturn is so often symbolized as an old man with a scythe. In the Qabalah the same thought is intimated by the attribution of Sanctifying Intelligence to the third Sephirah, inasmuch as a saint is a "just man made perfect." Thus, when we learn that Qabalists also call Binah the "Root of Water," we see that to this Sephirah they impute the power which gives concrete form to the spiritual potencies of the Life Power. This is the finitising power, or Salt, which is definitely associated with what the Chaldean Oracles call "the lustral water of the loud resounding Sea." For it must be remembered that even "fresh" water, like that in rivers and lakes, holds in solution minute quantities of salt, which are concentrated in sea water by the process of evaporation. Thus by our study of the Sephirah which is called the Sphere of Saturn, the Mother, the Great Sea, and the Root of Water, (and is also related in the *Aesch Mezareph* to alchemical Salt) we find many indications that alchemical Water is that aspect of the Life Power from which all things derive their forms. It is the Life Power in its aspect of substance, the principle of embodiment, as contrasted with the same Life Power in its aspect of energy, the principle of movement.

Now, in the alchemical system of the *Aesch Mezareph*, the element of water is also attributed to Chesed, the fourth Sephirah, and to Hod, the eighth Sephirah. The same system attributes Silver, or the Moon, to Chesed, and Copper, or Venus, to Hod. One has only to remember the connection of the Moon with the tides, and the astrological description of the Moon as cold and moist, to see how anything associated with Luna must be of the nature of water. Venus, too, is sea born, and you have read (Lesson Two, page 45) that the First Matter is called Venus, and also that it is called water.

Here you must be on your guard. If you have read our other writings dealing with the Tree of Life, you know that Chesed is designated as the Sphere of Jupiter, and that Hod is called the Sphere of Mercury. You have also been warned not to confuse the *sphere* of a planet with the planet itself. Thus when you read that alchemical water and the Moon are assigned to Chesed, and that the same element and Venus are assigned to Hod, this is what you should understand:

Water is the *substance* aspect of the First Matter, having its *root* in that which is represented on the Qabalistic Tree of Life as Binah, to which is attributed alchemical

Salt. This substance aspect also appears as the fourth Sephirah, hence in the Pattern on the Trestleboard we associate "Limitless Substance" with Chesed. In this particular manifestation of the Life Power, the alchemical water takes the *form* of "Silver" or "Luna," but this metaphysical Moon is at the same time the field or sphere in which the operation of the power designated as Jupiter is at work. Similarly the substance aspect of the First Matter presents itself in the eighth Sephirah under the *form* of alchemical Copper or Venus, and the latter is the field or sphere for the operation of the power called Mercury. These details will require careful consideration, but they are valuable clues to the right understanding of the whole mystery of alchemy.

Use as your guide throughout your Qabalistic and alchemical studies the key thought "All things are from One." That ONE presents itself under various aspects. The three primary aspects are: Mercury, corresponding to Kether, the Root of Air, and representing the *knowledge* aspect of the Life Power; Sulfur, corresponding to Chokmah, the Root of Fire, and representing the *activity* aspect of the Life Power; Salt, corresponding to Binah, the Root of Water, and representing the *substance* aspect of the Life Power. But these three are aspects of One Reality. They correspond to the omniscience (Mercury), omnipotence (Sulfur), and omnipresence (Salt) of Universal Spirit.

Thus our quotation from the *Turba Philosophorum* on page 123 within the previous pages says that the alchemical water owes its permanence to the fact that it is *united* to its Sulfur. The Sulfur is Chokmah, the Root of Fire, called Ab, the Father, in the Qabalah. Chokmah is the active Life Force, and without this active Life Force the substance aspect of the Life Power cannot endure. The alchemical water is the vehicle of the alchemical fire. The fire is hidden within it, and thus it is also written that the philosophers "burn with water."

The quotation on page 123 calls it a "tortured water, that hath suffered some alteration obvious to all, but known to few." In the picture of the hanged Man, the central figure is obviously undergoing a form of torture. Furthermore, the nature of that torture is suspension by a rope. Now, on page 130 you have read that the number of the letter Mem, forty, is the number of a Hebrew noun which means "rope" and also "pain, sorrow." But what is a rope, actually? A line composed of many *twisted* strands. And the verb "twist" is closely allied, by derivation, to the verb "torture." Modern science has shown definitely that the substance of all things is really a manifestation of electro-magnetic energy which is in a continual whirling, twisting motion. When this energy manifests as a flash of lightning, it assumes a spiral form, like an uncoiling rope. This fact was known to the ancients, for the Chaldean Oracles speak of the "spiral force" energized by the creative god. It was known, too, to the designers of the Tarot, and they selected the rope as part of the symbolism of the 12th Tarot Key in order to put that knowledge on record.

When it is said that the alchemical water has "suffered some alteration obvious to all, but known to few," the meaning is that this substance has assumed all the various forms, or embodiments, which are apparent even to the most ignorant of human kind. Thus the alteration is *obvious* to all. It is "known to few," because only a minority of the human beings alive in any generation perceive the unity of substance behind the multiplicity of appearances.

The permanence of the alchemical water is also hinted at in the attribution of *Stable Intelligence* to the letter Mem. And this Stable Intelligence is aid to be "the source of consistency among all the Sephiroth." Stability is immutability, soundness, vitality, coherence, solidity.

All these qualities are directly associated with the ideas of substance and permanence which are represented by alchemical water. Furthermore, the Hanged Man represents the idea of suspension, the state of a solid when its particles are mixed with, but undissolved in, a fluid. Thus the alchemists tell us that their water holds all things, like seeds in a bag. And in some versions of the Hanged Man, there is a bag tied behind the arms of the suspended figure, from which coins are dropping. This is a direct reference to the alchemical idea just stated.

The alchemical water, however, like ordinary water, has the power of dissolving substances as well as the power of holding them in suspension. Solution is the act or process whereby a substance is absorbed into, and homogeneously mixed with a liquid substance. This is the meaning of the alchemical term "dissolution," but this term is closely related also to that use of the word "dissolution" which is synonymous with "death." It is this aspect of alchemical water which is represented by the 13th Tarot Key.

This Key corresponds to the letter Nun, and the root idea of that letter is "to be full of seeds." This, of course, is in close correspondence to the alchemical teaching that the element of water is the "sperm of the world." Again, as an adjective, the word *Nun* means "permanence, or perpetuity," and this connects with the alchemical teaching that the element named water is a permanent fluid.

Dissolution is declared to be the great secret of the whole alchemical operation, and the 13th Key of the Tarot is symbolic of this arcanum. It is connected with the zodiacal sign Scorpio, a fixed sign of the watery quality, named עקרב, *Okareb*, in Hebrew. The number of this word is three hundred and seventy-two, and it is the number of the noun כבשים, *Kebeshim*, "young lambs;" of the noun עשב, "grass, herbage;" and of שבע, which has various pointings and meanings, including: 1) to be full, filled, satisfied; 2) abundance, plenty; 3) to swear, to bind with an oath; 4) the numeral seven.

"Young lambs" is a direct reference to the fiery quality hidden in alchemical water, for the lamb is an immature ram, and is therefore a symbol of the alchemical fire connected with Aries, the Ram.

"Grass" or "herbage" refers to the embodiment of life in physical form, and because of the profusion of seed in such herbage, is connected with the reproductive force represented by Scorpio, and with the symbol of the seed is the upper corner of the 13th Tarot Key. In Hebrew symbolism human life is also represented by grass, as in the phrase, "As for man, his days are as grass." Thus in the 13th Key, the skeleton reaper is mowing human hands, feet and heads. Furthermore, the seed symbol in that Key is in the corner of the picture corresponding to that in which is placed the symbol of the sign Aquarius (a man's head) in Keys 10 and 21. The intimation here is that alchemical water, the "Sperm of the world," is the substance which, as Eliphas Levi says, man seems to multiply in the reproduction of his species.

שבע, as meaning to be filled, to be satisfied, reminds us that this substance contains all that we can possibly desire for the satisfaction of every need. As meaning to swear, to *bind with an oath*, the same word hints that our use of this power entails certain definite obligations. Thus Eliphas Levi says of the Hanged Man, who represents another phase of the same alchemical water, "He is the adept, bound by his engagements." In every occult school the aspirant must take certain definite obligations, and the answer to the Masonic interrogation, "What makes you a Mason?" is, "My obligation." Finally, שבע, as representing the number Seven, indicates a point definitely connected with the alchemical water, since the latter is said to be the "seed of the metals," which are seven in number.

In the Tarot the number Seven is also connected with the element of water, because it is the number of the Key called The Chariot, which corresponds to the watery sign Cancer. The idea of *fluidity* is also connected with the name of the Qabalistic path connected with this 7th Key, for that path is called "The Intelligence of the House of *Influence*."

The letter corresponding to the sign Cancer is Cheth, the Enclosed Field. Note that the idea of enclosure harks back to that of limitation, associated with Saturn. The enclosed field is what Hindu philosophy calls the *Kshetra*, which is the name given in the *Bhagavad Gita* to "this body." "Kshetra" means literally "the perishable" and also "the field." The entire 13th chapter of the Gita is an exposition of the relation between the Kshetra (the Chariot) and the Kshetrajna, or consciousness (the Charioteer). All objects whatsoever are included in the Kshetra, which is the same as Prakriti, the "mysterious power," or the finitising principle.

In Hebrew, the sign Cancer is named סרטן = 319 = ישׁט, and the latter is a verb signifying, "to stretch out, to extend." Here is an intimation that the aspect of alchemical water presented by Cheth, the sign Cancer, and Key Seven is that of *expansion* or *extension*. The fundamental idea is that the alchemical water is that which forms itself into all manner of objects. It is the principle, too, of increase and augmentation. In physics, the term extension is defined as "that property of a body by which it occupies a portion of space." This connects directly, also, with astrological meanings of the sign Cancer, which is the natural fourth house sign in a horoscope, having to do with landed property, real estate, home, and the like. In horary astrology, moreover, this sign and its house represents the "end of the matter," or the completion of a cycle of manifestation, which completion has to do with the notion of perfection, increase, and development. These, of course, are fundamental ideas represented by the number seven.

One other Hebrew letter corresponds to water, the letter Qoph, whose name means "back of the head." Here is a subtlety that escapes many. The "head" is a technical term of Qabalah meaning the number one, and Kether, which is the Sephirah corresponding to the beginning of manifestation. Qoph, the *back* of the head, stands for that which is *behind* this beginning. *Behind* it may be understood as meaning "prior to it," and also as signifying "underlying motivation." In our common speech we refer to our hidden motives when we say of a person whose intentions are not quite clear to us, "I wish I knew what is in the back of his head."

The Qabalah gives us a very definite clue as to the hidden motivation of the cosmic process of manifestation when it assigns the Corporeal Intelligence to the letter Qoph. Concerning this the *Book of Formation* says: "The twenty-ninth path is called the Corporeal Intelligence, so called because it forms every body which is formed in all the worlds, and the reproduction of them." In other words, the hidden motive for manifestation is the formation and reproduction of bodies which shall serve as adequate vehicles for expressing the inner potencies of the Life Power. Hermetic doctrine is the same, for it says that the One Force is "integrating, if it be turned into earth."

That this power of integration is directly associated with water may be seen in the Tarot Key corresponding to Qoph, Key Eighteen, The Moon. For there the path of the Corporeal Intelligence begins in a pool of water, and ends on the snowy height occupied by the Hermit in Key Nine. The snow and ice of the Hermit's environment are crystallized, or solidified water. Thus the path of Key Eighteen begins in *fluid* and ends in *solid* water. It is the path of the fixation of the volatile, as an alchemist would say.

Qoph corresponds to the water sign Pisces, named דגים, *Dagim*, in Hebrew. דגים = 57, and this is the number of several Hebrew words that shed light on what the alchemists understood by water. First of all, it should be noted that fifty-seven is one of the multiples of the very significant Qabalistic number, nineteen, which owes its importance to the fact that it is the value of the name חוה, Eve. As a verb Chaveh means "to manifest, to show forth," and thus refers to the power of manifestation associated with water in alchemy.

Frederick Bligh Bond has shown that nineteen is also important in Greek Gematria. It is a factor in the values of the following words: Η ΓΗ, He Ge, the Earth, 1 x 19; Η ΤΑΙΑ ΘΕΑ, He Gaia Thea, The Earth Goddess, 2 x 19; ΑΘΗΝΗ, Athene, the Virgin Goddess, 4 x 19; ΜΑΡΙΑ, Mary, 8 x 19; Η ΜΗΝΗ, He Mene, the Moon, 6 x 19.

The first word corresponding to fifty-seven is אבדן, signifying "destruction." This corresponds to what is said of the First Matter, which, you will remember is identified with water, in the earlier lesson; "It is set up for the ruin of many and the salvation of some."

The participle, אוכל, eating, or consuming, also has the value of fifty-seven. This relates to the idea that alchemical water has the power of apparently devouring form. The Scriptures tell us that God is a devouring or consuming fire, and you have learned that alchemists say that they *burn* with water.

Another correspondence to fifty-seven is the word און, *On*. In one reading it means nothingness, vanity, falsehood, wickedness, injustice. Differently pointed it signifies strength, power, wealth, substance; but also, affliction, pain. These meanings would be very significant to any one well versed in esoteric astrology, since they correspond to the positive and negative manifestations of the sign Pisces, and of the twelfth house in the horoscope, corresponding to that sign.

But fifty-seven is also the number of the verb בנה, Baneh, to build, to form, to erect, to raise, to establish, to restore, and all these meanings are directly connected with what has been said concerning the Corporeal Intelligence associated with Qoph and the zodiacal sign Pisces.

Again, fifty-seven is the number of מזבח, altar. The suggestion here is that since what the alchemists mean by "water" is the source of form, or embodiment, it is also that in which inheres the principle of sacrifice. To this may be related the injunction of St. Paul, "Present your bodies a living sacrifice." This is exactly what the alchemical process amounts to. He who understands what is really accomplished by alchemy, or by its Oriental equivalent, yoga, realizes that the Great Work is the perfection of the human vehicle by the sacrifice of all that prevents it from being a completely transparent medium for the expression of the potencies of the Life Power.

Summing all this up, we may understand that alchemical fire and alchemical water are not two things, but one, manifest in opposite directions. Alchemical fire is the activity, or Sulfur, aspect of the One Reality. Alchemical water is the substance, or Salt, aspect of the same thing. The triangle representing fire points upward. That representing water points downward, to indicate the integrating, building, manifesting, or form producing activity of the One Reality.

Alchemical water is that aspect of the One Thing which, as the *Emerald Tablet* says, "receives the power of the superiors and of the inferiors." It is the aspect of the Life Power upon which the One Conscious Energy broods, to bring forth forms. For us it is the substance of our bones, our flesh, our blood. It is the subtle *fluid* called electro-magnetism by modern physicists, and its most important manifestations are in our nerves, our veins, our arteries, and our lymphatic ducts. Its currents through our nervous system are directly influenced, shaped and formed by our mental imagery. Thus modified, these currents affect the vital secretions, and so change the chemistry of the blood and lymph.

Thus Mrs. Atwood says:

> Alchemy is the universal art of vital chemistry, which by fermenting the human spirit, purifies, and, finally dissolving it, opens the elementary germ into new life and consciousness; and the Philosopher's Stone is the efflux of such a life, drawn to a focus and made manifest as a concrete Essence of Light, which Essence is the true Form or Idea of Gold. The process takes place in and through the human body in the blood, changing the relation of its component parts and principles.

The same idea is told in the Rosicrucian allegory of the *Fama Fraternitatis*. There we are told that Brother C.R. was initiated in the "Temple of Dam-Car," or "Temple of the Blood of the Lamb," after he had spent some time in Damascus, by reason of the infirmity of his body. "Damascus" means "work," and Brother C.R.'s sojourn there has to do with the work of purification made necessary by the physical imperfections which must be overcome by what alchemists call the "gross work." This must be undertaken before the "subtle work" may be attempted with any degree of safety.

It is because occult students are so often not properly instructed as to the necessity of this "gross work" that so many cranks are to be found amongst them. They attempt the subtle work with bodies unprepared. The inevitable consequence, even of such supposedly safe practices as meditation and other forms of Raja Yoga, is a subtle distribution of poisons throughout the body.

No error is more common than the supposition that it is safe to undertake mental practice without preliminary physical preparation. This error is found in the writings of many teachers who, it would seem, ought to know better. Raja Yoga practice, meditation, visualization, and other forms of mental practice are just as physical as any other bodily activity. They involve the subtle currents of alchemical water in the brain and nervous system. Nothing is more dangerous, if begun before the organism has been purified. Of all the insidious efforts of what occultists know as the "black forces," none is more deadly than the well meant attempts of many admirable persons to persuade their pupils to concentrate, meditate, visualize, and so on, without paying any attention to the preliminary "gross work." Some even go so far as to assert that the gross work was accomplished during our incarnation in earlier races, so that we need not attempt it now.

Tarot gives pertinent hints to the contrary. The 12th Key, representing alchemical water itself, emphasizes our personal dependence upon the cosmic tree of existence, upon the physical laws determining personality. Key Thirteen has to do with the functions of the reproductive and genito-urinary organs. Key Seven relates to the stomach. Key Eighteen is connected with the total body consciousness. Thus all the emphasis of the Tarot Keys representing the element of water falls upon the physical embodiment of the Life Power in our organism, upon the need for right selection of food, upon the need of controlling and sublimating the force working through the genito-urinary organs, and finally, upon the need for a clear recognition of the truth that the path into the region of the higher consciousness is a path of physiological transformation.

Alchemical water, then, is the cosmic fire, specialized in the nerve currents and chemistry of the blood stream. The purification of this water must be the first work of the alchemist. He must choose true foods, and regulate his habits of eating. He must control his sex life, and see that kidney elimination is what it should be. Finally, he must learn, little by little, to rebuild his body, sacrificing everything that clouds or obscures its transparency to the Light of the Life Power, and imposing a pattern of the New Image upon its cells through the agency of the subconscious mind.

MAGIC THAT WORKS
FROM ANCIENT MASTERS TO MODERN SEEKERS
FRANCES HARRISON AND NINEVEH SHADRACH

Possibilities are endless when it comes to authentic magic that can transform your life like never before. Ancient masters practiced a system of magic rooted in objective reality of spiritual forces and with their aid they performed many miracles. Those secrets lay shrouded in the stories of The Arabian Nights and King Solomon. A fraction of their teachings made it to the West via Moorish Spain and influenced the occult renaissance of Europe. Magic That Works goes back to those original sources of obscure grimoires and hard to find manuscripts to present a practical system based on ancient Middle Eastern paganism of the Chaldeans and Sabians, and traditional Jewish and Arabic magic, adapted for modern Westerners to use.

Packed with beneficial methods and techniques, Magic That Works is an alternative for solitary magical work from the ground up for spiritual transformation and personal empowerment. Apply those ancient keys to the elements, planets, angels and jinn toward:

· Quickly contacting your holy guardian angel and unveiling your spiritual destiny
· Unleashing Elemental forces to gain true self-mastery and benefiting yourself and others
· Opening spiritual gateways to alternate planes and attracting beneficial forces to your life.
· Channeling the power of the ancient planets and learning how to shape your own astrological reality
· Calling on spiritual jinn with ancient incantations to help you in your spiritual and mundane affairs
· Applying advanced techniques for attaining wisdom, psychic protection, healing, and blessing.

Whether you are a total beginner or an advanced Magus, this book will help catapult your magical development to whole new levels. You can start doing now what most people only dream about and make a difference in your life and the lives of your loved ones. If you are looking for authentic magic that is tested, effective, safe, totally in the Light, and produces tangible results, you should try the techniques in this book — the title will speak for itself.

0973593121 paperback 360 pages $24.95

MYSTICAL MEDITATIONS ON THE CHRISTIAN COLLECTS

DION FORTUNE

Mystical Meditations on the Collects is a collection of esoteric explanations of the prayers in the Anglican Church Book of Prayers. These prayers are offered during the church calendar to honor saints and holy days. An accomplished occultist and deep mystic, Dion Fortune shares gems of perception through her brilliant commentaries. Her interpretation of these prayers provides a bridge between the Christian faith and the mystical traditions and gives guidance to those who truly wish to live lives modeled upon the Master Jesus.

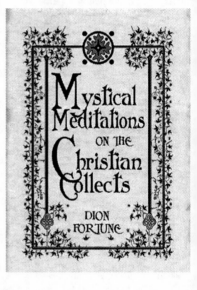

The mysticism that inspires these meditations transcends their Christian origins, to be of a universal order that recognizes the underlying truth of all religions. The insights in Miss Fortune's analysis contain treasures for any devout person, Christian or otherwise. If you love to be inspired by great spiritual wisdom, you will love this book.

0978053419 paperback 188 pages $15.95

INNER AND OUTER ORDER INITIATIONS OF THE HOLY ORDER OF THE GOLDEN DAWN

ARTHUR EDWARD WAITE

The initiations of the Order of the Fellowship of the Rosy Cross and the Holy Order of the Golden Dawn constitute an important part of the Golden Dawn tradition. After close to 80 years, they have been published and are now accessible for all the students of the Golden Dawn tradition. They are important not only due to their historical relevance, but also because of their strong Rosicrucian influence and focus on the combining of magic with the path of love and compassion. They are beautifully written, moving, and make for excellent GD ritual magic. Those

familiar with Waite's style of writing will be happy to know that the rites are almost devoid of Waite's loquaciousness. They are without doubt some of the finest writing this famous occultist has ever produced. Now, for the first time in more than 80 years, these secret ceremonies of the Fellowship of the Rosy Cross are revealed and made available to YOU.

0973593172 hardback 336 pages $55.95

CODEX OF LOVE
SACRED TEACHINGS FROM
THE QUEEN OF HEAVEN

CODEX OF LOVE brings the message of the Goddess to Her children with words sweeter than honey and more addictive than chocolate.

Unprecedented in the history of our modern world is a direct revelation from the Queen of Heaven. The religion of Ilu Ishtar is one of the world oldest and has left its marks on many parts of the world.

History comes alive with this revelation, which was accompanied with miraculous physical signs. Even though the hands that recorded the book chose to remain anonymous, the message speaks for itself. Elegant and deceptively simple, it contains the missing teachings of heaven.

Feel the energy as you read it out loud to yourself and be ready to be amazed by the profound sense of love that surrounds you. You will want to read it again and again.

Whispers of rituals and Goddess mysteries will beckon to you from between the lines. A tantalizing journey of discovery awaits those called to explore and uncover the hidden meanings of the Goddess's own holy book.

0973593113 paperback 236 pages $15.95

COMING SOON

AJNAS KING SOLOMON'S OCCULT HANDBOOK
ACCORDING TO HIS PERSONAL SEER
ASAPH BEN BERECHIAH

Direct translation from Arabic and Hebrew one of the rarest grimoires of the ancient world. It is a collection of Solomonic magic of spiritual and sublime nature. It deals with the sacred and holy names of the planets and angels. It contains more than seven evocations to Metatron alone. It also details complete magical information on King Solomon's magic of the princes of the jinn. Areas covered on jinn magic include the construction of the magical ring, the magical carpet, the inscription on the altar slab and much more. This is one of the most important theurgical books on magic since the first translation of the Greater Key of Solomon and the Magic of the Abramelin the Mage.

JINN SUMMONING
ARCANE COMPENDIUM FOR THE ADVANCED MAGICIAN
NINEVEH SHADRACH

Culled from dozens of Arabic manuscripts and books, this is the complete compendium of jinn evocations known to date. Many of the conjurations were guarded by oral traditions and by masters and remain virtually unknown to the modern Western world. Included are numerous classical methods of summoning jinn to direct manifestation, as well as methods of scrying in the magical mirror. This book is not for beginners looking to learn the ABCs of magical evocation, but for advanced adepts looking to duplicate the miracles recorded in ancient grimoires that so far have eluded modern occultists. Novice magicians should only use the materials in this book under guidance of an experienced master.

Printed in the United States
131206LV00001B/37/A

9 780978 053512